Magdalene's
TIMELESS
TESTAMENT

ROLLING AWAY THE STONE
UNCOVERING TRUTH

Judith Grant

Still Small Voice
Publishing

Magdalene's
TIMELESS TESTAMENT
-ROLLING AWAY THE STONE
-UNCOVERING TRUTH

by Judith Grant

Library of Congress Control Number: 2002110547
ISBN: 0-9722622-2-9

This book is printed in the United States of America

To my dearest friend and partner,

Patricia Madigan Stringham

Who taught us that love, compassion and being fully present in the moment are the instruments of healing as we journey to discover our own truth.

Acknowledgements

It was a difficult decision to publish this book. Channeling had initially challenged my beliefs and it took some time before I embraced this beautiful method of communication with our spiritual guidance. Another dilemma that I faced was, "If I am channeling the book, who is the author?" Certainly it was my free will that accepted the words, but they belong to a woman of great inner strength and unshakable faith in God. I am thankful for Mary Magdalene's timeless messages of Love.

None of this material would have been brought forward if it were not for the teachings, guidance, and encouragement of my partner, Dr. William Bezmen. His experience in the field of psycho-spirituality as well as his insight recognized the phenomena as it began to unfold. Through his mentorship, both Pattie and I were able to learn how to get out of our own way and trust the messages we were receiving. William was always there, conducting the channeling sessions while providing us all with a sense of peace and safety. He always had the patience to answer all my left brain questions and did so from a place of not only intellect, but of a loving and deep faith.

Patricia Madigan Stringham, was in humanity and is in spiritual essence, my closest and dearest friend. From the moment we met, words were never needed to express what was in our hearts. We held fast to our beliefs and each other during those early challenging days and she will be forever with me. As it was 2000 years ago, so it will be again, dear friend.

I would like to acknowledge now, Ed Stringham. This book would not be in print if it were not for his devotion, courage and love. He spent countless hours of transcribing the channeled tapes, months of collaboration with William and I in organizing the material. I am grateful for his writing of the foreword, afterword and commentaries. This has been in addition to actually publishing this book. My heart is full of love and gratitude for all that he has done to bring a dream into a reality.

There are two special women that I wish to thank and honor at this time. Roseanne Tiffany and Julie Nittoli donated many, many hours of editing in order to punctuate the transcribed material and place it into a readable text. I thank them for their patience and honor their friendship. I also would like to thank our friends, students, and clients for their attendance and support of the channeled sessions.

Words cannot fully express my love and appreciation for my children Dawn, Nicole, and Christopher and grandchildren Amanda, Katelyn, and Jacob who have all been the greatest gift and accomplishment of my lifetime. To Russell Grant a special thank you for all his love and support as I have been walking this path.

Contents

Foreword

There are many things in my reality which I find incomprehensible, such as electricity. I can explain it to you as it was taught to me but I still don't really understand it. The analogy I use to express my comprehension of channeling is that of the radio, which I understand about as well as I do electricity. I can't see radio waves yet I experience their presence. Somewhere, there is an unseen transmitter that converts thoughts, expressed as sounds, into waves of energy and sends them to a receiver that recreates and amplifies the sounds for the listener. Strange, even magical, but I accept it every day.

My definition of channeling is based on direct experience, both as a receiver and as a witness. Understand that at first I was very skeptical and had witnessed "channelers" whose performances I questioned. Any time there is the possibility of making money or fooling people there will be charlatans and channeling is no different. All human endeavors provide examples of deceit and even what has passed for science has had its fakirs.

Although incomplete, my view of channeling is as follows: thoughts are energy and physicists have told us that energy can neither be created nor destroyed. Science tells us, however, that energy can be transformed. In one human lifetime, millions of thoughts are generated between birth and death. These thoughts, which are energy exist, *but where?* In our physical reality some are evident and given expression through our actions. Sometimes, they stay within us and become part of our inner life. At the death of the body these thoughts are not destroyed with the flesh; consciousness continues. This collection of thoughts persists and exists *somewhere*. When another human life comes into existence, with a similar internal makeup, or frequency, those energy thought forms have now found a sympathetic receiver. This receiver/channeler is analogous to a radio which can tune to specific frequencies. The receiver can choose to ignore them and shut off any attempt to hear and play these messages. However, by choosing to "listen", one becomes a more skilled receiver. Some develop the ability to tune in, like a radio, to a variety of frequencies.

Those who start to channel often battle their own concept that they are losing their mental hold on reality because channeling is not currently accepted by our western cultural matrix. This was not always so. In the Old Testament, God instructed the Jews to build a tabernacle. Within the most sacred inner space, the Holy of Holies, they kept the Ark of the Covenant. This ark had been constructed according to instructions from God. Because part of those instructions are recorded in the Old Testament, some have suggested that this ark was a primitive radio receiver. God spoke to the priests through this Ark and those messages were then given to the faithful.

As time went by there were prophets who claimed to have a special gift to hear the Word of God. In a sense, they became receivers/channelers of God's thoughts and messages. Jesus taught that we each have within us the innate ability to hear God and discern truth. He taught that by looking within (meditation), we connect to a direct link that needs no intermediary. This belief was held by fellow Jews in Galilee in Jesus' time. Is it possible that humans have always had the spiritual capacity to communicate in this manner? Jesus' teachings seem to say just that. Is this not a form of channeling?

Most Christians who I know seem to believe that God stopped communicating directly with man once the Old and New Testaments were written. Anyone who is interested in theology and reads about the compilation of the Bible we use today, knows that it contains contradictory reports of the same incidents. These contradictions can be the result of human error. Many Biblical scholars claim that the Synoptic Gospels were most likely written after the deaths of the original apostles. Finally, we know that around 325AD, at the Council of Nicea, many of the early writings were "lost" or intentionally removed from the collection for various reasons, some of them political. It is possible that the Holy Bible, as we know it may be fallible and incomplete? Wouldn't God want all of his children to have access to the truth and guidance that they need? It is my belief that God would find other routes to send the needed messages and that channeling can be one of those avenues.

Magdalene's TIMELESS TESTAMENT

Since I have seen and personally experienced channeling it has become part of my reality.   I believe what is written here for I have seen it manifested and I know the integrity of those who are the messengers.

Ed Stringham

Introduction

One of the basic premises presented in this book is "What you choose to believe is up to you." If your only acid test for truth is a variation of the scientific method, you may well miss much useful information and experience. The material presented in this book, which was channeled, is this type of information.

How do we know what is true? New information can be compared to existing information and a choice can be made. The information that has been gleaned from the Dead Sea Scrolls since the 1940's has impacted the doctrines handed down by various authorities of the Christian Church. Sometimes there was agreement, sometimes there was not. These "new" old documents raised many questions as to what was true about Jesus, or Yeshua, as Mary Magdalene calls him. How does one decide what is truth? Does truth come from some "authority" outside the questioner or does the questioner have deep within his own being the capability of knowing what is truth?

The message brought by the Magdalene in this book repeatedly states that the seeker has the God given ability to discern truth. Let not the reader assume that this is just another new age, feel good, and everything is wonderful type of presentation. A true seeker will encounter issues and ideas here that are just the opposite of taking the easy path. A crucial decision in reading this material and deciding on its veracity is whether or not you believe or can conceive that the spark of God is within you. If you can believe that you have the God energy within your being then you can determine what is truth.

There are many who must believe that direct spiritual information and "knowing" existed only in the Old and New Testaments. Does that make sense? Would a God who had revealed himself and universal truths decide that no further communication was needed during the past 2000 years? That does not seem likely. Creation and evolution are ongoing processes and information has proved, in all other areas of our reality, not to be the "final word." Would the realm of spirit be any different?

Each soul has its own perspective, tempered by its unique life experiences, both past and present. Mary Magdalene is no different. While the basic facts might be shared and agreed upon by several witnesses to an event, the importance and impact of each of those things experienced is unique to each soul. We first let the Magdalene present herself so that the reader can understand as much about her as possible. The readings reveal a personality with much more depth than the little we read in the New Testament or the stories that are part of the Church myth/history. The strength of the Magdalene comes through, as does her uncompromising honesty. Nowhere is she taken with her own role as one who is close to Jesus. In transcribing the sessions this was a surprise since one might have expected a little self-importance to come through.

As Mary Magdalene walked her life journey, Jesus appeared and she followed. It was simple and straightforward. Nor is there judgment, even of those who made the journey more difficult. The elimination of judgement, both of others and ourselves, is a concept repeatedly stressed in this book. As I became more familiar with the material, I wondered if Mary perceived what was happening around her at that time with the same non-judgemental clarity as she presents to us now. Or is this the gift a soul receives from distance and spiritual growth? I don't yet have that answer.

Ed Stringham

The Couriers

This book is the collaborative effort of four individuals. In introducing them let it be known that we had the following in common:

- We were unknown to each other in this current life time
- Our coming together seemed to be serendipitous
- We were not seeking this information
- We each questioned, wrestled, and agonized over the information as it was brought to us
- In the beginning, the messages came as pieces of a puzzle, isolated and disjointed
- As time passed, the puzzle began to fill in and we came not only to accept it but felt compelled to share this story.

In 1993, while teaching clinical hypnotherapy in western New York, Dr. William Bezmen met Patricia and Ed Stringham, who were two students in his class. In the years that followed he remained a teacher, colleague and friend. During that same period I met Dr. Bezmen at SUNY at Stony Brook Graduate School of Nursing where he was teaching a course on alternative modalities of healing. I continued to study meditation and hypnotherapy with Dr. Bezmen on Long Island. In 1995, the channelled information in this book started to come through to Patricia and I even though we lived four hundred miles apart. William, recognizing the importance of this information, brought us together.

The four individuals that formed the collaborative team are:

- **William Bezmen is the facilitator of the channeling sessions.** Dr. Bezmen holds a Fellow in Clinical Hypnotherapy and is a Clinical Specialist in Psychiatric Nursing. For over twenty five years William has been in private practice on Long Island, New York. His practice includes the treatment of patients and the development and teaching of hypnosis and spirituality courses. William is co-owner and director of Pathways to Health, an integrative healing and education center on Long Island, New York.

- **Judith Grant is the vehicle of the Magdalene spirit and author of this book.**- Judith has a Masters in Nursing Science from SUNY at Stony Brook and maintains a certification in Oncology Nursing from the Oncology Nursing Society. She is currently certified as both an Adult and Geriatric Nurse Practitioiner. As co-owner and director of Pathways to Health, Judith teaches and lectures extensively on spirituality, the healing arts, and integrative medicine.

- **Patricia Madigan Stringham is the vehicle of the Mary of Bethany spirit**. Patricia held a Masters in Psychology and was a certified child psychologist and school administrator. She earned her Doctorate in Clinical Hypnotherapy in 1995. Pattie was a co-owner of Pathways to Health and had a private counseling practice for adults and children. Patricia transitioned into light on December 9, 1999.

- **Ed Stringham, husband of Pattie, is the transcriber of the Magdalene tapes. He is also commentator and publisher of this book.** Ed holds a degree in Architecture and a Master's in Industrial Design. He was professor of Industrial Modelmaking and owns and operates a prototype fabrication business. Ed also holds certification in Clinical Hypnosis.

The Beginning

As the author, I thought it important that the reader be given information regarding the journey that let to the writing of this book. Dr. William Bezmen played a key role from the very beginning. I asked him to share, with the reader, his account of those early days.

Dr. William Bezmen: In the spring of 1994 I received a phone call from one of my students who lived in upstate New York. Her name was Patricia Madigan Stringham. Pattie was noticeably upset and told me that she was frightened. All of my previous experience with Pattie proved that she was a well-grounded professional who could easily handle stressful situations. Her being upset was very out of character. She explained to me that she was experiencing visions during her mediations that were startling because they seemed so real. She was repeatedly having visions of two women listening to a discussion between three men on a hillside which seemed to be the Middle East. What was particularly upsetting to her was that one of the men appeared to be Jesus. I encouraged Pattie to journal the details of her visions and meditations. At her request I shared this information with no one.

During the same period of time, I was teaching an advanced meditation class on Long Island. Judith, a student in that class, spoke to me about visions that she was experiencing during my guided journeys. She was initially upset because regardless of where I was leading the group she kept ending up in the same place. It was an ancient village outside of what appeared to be Jerusalem. This continued to happen over the next few weeks. I encouraged her to journal these experiences in detail. One day, Judith shared a journal entry with me that was so similar to Pattie's experiences that it startled me and it could not be ignored. They both described the same event from the perspective of the two women sitting on the hillside. Pattie, from the perspective of a woman identified as Mary of Bethany; and Judith from the perspective of Mary Magdalene. In their journals, Pattie and Judith both identified one of the three men as Jesus. My years of experience with past life regression convinced me they were channeling information from a similar past life. To further explore this phenomenon, it was necessary for these two women to meet. When I brought them together there was an immediate and powerful connection.

The three of us began to work together, and under my guidance, Judith and Pattie were able to revisit and further explore that event. Over a period of time, they began to full trance channel the two women. We learned that Mary of Bethany was the wife of Jesus, and the mother of his three children, and Mary Magdalene was his devoted apostle and friend. Information continued to be presented to us about the life of the man we know as Jesus, as well as his followers. As this was unfolding, a powerful bond and commitment developed between the three of us. We also believed intuitively that there were others who had latent memories of that time, and this soon proved to be true. The three of us opened an integrative healing center called Pathways to Health. The messages we were receiving were so powerful and healing that they needed to be shared. This book is a compilation of fifteen, one and half-hour audio taped channeling sessions for the public that I facilitated between 1997 and 2001.

William Bezmen

As William described, this incredible journey began for me, in a meditation class. My purpose in attending this class was to learn techniques of relaxation, both for myself and my cancer patients. Little did I know what was about to unfold! What transpired defied my logical and analytical mind. I had no prior interest in, or experience with past life regression or channeling. The first time I met the Magdalene in a meditative vision, there was a lot of disbelief and self doubt on my part. I needed to make sense of what was occurring. With a Master's in Nursing Science and my Catholic upbringing, these experiences did not fit into my belief system. What I had been taught of Mary Magdalene was that she was the adulteress / sinner healed by Jesus, and she was the one who found the tomb empty after His death. I have grown to understand The Magdalene to be, in truth, a woman of deep faith, commitment and compassion. She walked with Jesus and his disciples as an equal.

I met Pattie after sharing my unusual experiences with William. He told me that there was someone I needed to meet who lived in upstate New York. Soon after, he arranged that meeting.

There are no words to describe what I felt when our eyes first met. Patricia Madigan Stringham was the woman I repeatedly saw in my visions. She was the one I called Mary; the one I called friend. I don't remember taking my next breath. It was as though time stood still; as though time did not exist at all. On seeing me, Pattie jumped to her feet as startled as I, and called me Miriam. We talked for hours and compared our journal entries; *page after page, people, conversations, places and events, all described in the same way.* I could no longer reason away these experiences. I began to accept that what was occurring was beyond my human comprehension.

During the time when Pattie, William and I channeled privately, we asked many questions of The Magdalene and Mary of Bethany. We sought clarity and the truth of what really happened almost 2000 years ago. We asked, "What were the true teachings of Jesus? What messages did he bring at that time that could help this planet heal now?" These are the messages that we felt needed to be brought forward at this time.

Pattie and I have been asked whether or not we believe that we are the full reincarnations of Mary of Bethany and Mary Magdalene. I can answer for both of us - absolutely not! During the years of channeling, we came to understand that a human being does not reincarnate as the whole person that he or she once was. Instead, a soul can return with parts of memories of other consciousness that lived at other times. Perhaps there is unfinished work to be done, or universal messages that need to be brought forth. Some of us, as in the case of Pattie and I, tap into those parts of ourselves and allow the deep memories which are never lost, to surface.

There are different ways that people channel. One can listen to the channeled consciousness and repeat what is heard. Another way is to expand one's consciousness to a level of high vibration or frequency and with free will allow the consciousness to speak through the physical body. I channel one of my other guides, Balistar, in this latter way. With The Magdalene, however, it is completely different. I can feel my heart open and expand as the warmth and loving consciousness of Mary rises from deep within me.

The decision to publish this book was a difficult one. It took a great leap of faith for all of us to step beyond our professional boundaries. We were compelled to stand in the face of fear and to bring this information forward.

The choice to include the information presented during the channeling session which occurred on September 13, 2001 was not made lightly. Part of that session is transcribed in the last chapter of this book. I felt strongly that it was important to include the words of the Magdalene as they were spoken in response to the tragic events of September 11, 2001.

We trust that as people are drawn to read these **Timeless Messages**, it will help to ignite the Divine Light within them, raise their consciousness and fill them with the love and compassion that Jesus brought to humanity. In the words of The Magdalene, our purpose in humanity is to *remember* and to live that which, in truth, we are: "One Light, One Heart, One Love".

Her message is one of compassion and love. These are tools that can stop acts of hatred and fear. Our choice is either to be ruled by rage and retaliation or rise to a higher spiritual level to create a world where all are connected and valued. It is not a new message. Perhaps the time has come to renew our own connection to Divinity and begin to recognize the Divine Light in all living things.

Reader please note:

The words of Mary that came through the channeling sessions were minimally edited since we wanted to present the material in as pure a form as possible. The result of this decision means that the reader will find material that can -

- *start abruptly without introduction or transition*
- *be presented as long run on sentences like flows of consciousness, and*
- *sometimes be repetitive*

The commentaries written by Ed Stringham are italicized, as well as the questions asked of Mary Magdalene and Mary of Bethany. All channeled material is preceded and followed by three stars   * * *

At the end of this book, is an appendix indicating the dates of the channeled sessions.

Judith Grant.

CHAPTER ONE

Mary on Channeling

"In truth, as we ascend, as our soul and spirit reunites into the consciousness of Universal Light it expands beyond like those facets I spoke of. Each facet sees through the eyes of that reality, of that dimension, of that time. As we expand part of our awareness settles in different layers, vibrational frequencies, some higher than others. This is true with all that is channeled and brought back to your humanity."

The collaborators on this book have presented their experiences with channeling, both as witnesses and as channels. Mary gives us an expanded and more spiritual view on how and why channeling is possible.

Sparks of the Divine

* * *

There are sparks of Light coming from a great source of Light from the Eternal One and those sparks set out into the universe and often choose to experience something else, to learn, to grow.   Other sparks of Light remain in the universe as guardians and way-seers.   There are parts of our soul that have bits of that Light that lived in other lifetimes, parts of the memories, parts of the purpose.   It is really not as difficult to understand as some make it to be.   There are many here who have pieces and parts of those memories; they can feel it, the gentle stirring.   Sometimes with overwhelming passion and sometimes there is overwhelming grief.   Memories of other lifetimes also reside within each soul if it has journeyed again, memories of other teachers, of other experiences.   We are brought together to remember once again and to learn (B)

* * *

Channeled Information Can Be Distorted

When humans hear or read information and relay it to other humans, the possibility for distortion is

Mary On Channeling

very real. Channeled information, because it comes through humans, is no different. The "ring of truth" is an innate ability that each of us can cultivate. It is the final personal authority of what is true for each of us. Mary answers the question, "Is there distortion in channeling?"

* * *

Yes, distortion of information can occur through channeling. So what we bring to you and what you already know, and have heard so many times before, is to turn to that which is pure Light within you. As the guardians and guides of Light speak to you listen through the Light of your soul and you will hear truth. You will vibrate to that which is truth. The pure essence will reach out and expand beyond all expanding when truth is spoken to you. Have you not already begun to feel and recognize what is truth? It sings within you. So whether or not you are guided to the writings written in the hands of humanity, or whether you are brought by the guardians of Light to dimensions, many dimensions, layer upon layer, to view all from different perspectives, know that through the Light of the Christed consciousness, of that of which he spoke of is how you will know what is real.

* * *

Dr. Bezmen asks, "When other people channel information from Mary Magdalene, are these parts of her soul?"

* * *

In truth, as we ascend, as our soul and spirit reunites into the consciousness of Universal Light it expands beyond like those facets I spoke of. Each facet sees through the eyes of that reality, of that dimension, of that time. As we expand, part of our awareness settles in different layers, vibrational frequencies, some higher than others. This is true with all that is channeled and brought back to your humanity. Many can bring a fragment of that truth. What I dare say now is that it is up to the humanity of that which vibrates with that energy, to step aside of itself. Judge not what is being spoken and to allow the essence to move through, even if it does not align with the beliefs of the one who channels. Very often humanity will move what is being brought to it to meet its belief systems, to be comfortable with the information at hand, passing it through the filters and facets of what has been collected in this humanity. I ask each one who listens to all that is channeled, to all the consciousness of the universe, to listen without ears. Feel with your heart. Does it beat in the rhythm of that which is coming to you? How does your heart beat? Where does your soul take you? Does it bring you back in the sands of time? Do you feel his love? Does your soul remember what "she" (the channel) speaks? Ask this each time you hear the words and bring into your heart those fragments as you say, those pieces that fit the crystal within you.

* * *

Dr. Bezmen asks, "Mary, you recently wrote a message to Mary of Bethany through your host. Are we to give that to her? (Pattie, who brought the memories of Mary of Bethany forward, was enduring the effects of a terminal illness.)

* * *

She already knows that it is coming. It is the humanity that needs to hear the words. It is to that part that is still connected to the denser energy of this life that needs to know that she is not alone, that there is a part far greater that dwells within her, that is always with us. For in truth all that walk in the Light with him continue to be with one another and we are never alone, this promise he gave us, this promise he has kept. Our aloneness is in our forgetting, our joy is in our remembering. Surrender to it. Fear the forgetfulness, embrace the remembering. This is what she must know for now she feels alone so I speak to the part of her that remembers. (F)

* * *

From Spirit to Channeler

The memories that come to one who channels are often incomplete and their retrieval through the human mind can happen very quickly or slowly.

* * *

The transition was very slow in coming. There was much that I gathered, much to speak of. There is time of taking a moment and as you gather what is necessary to speak, and decide what is of little importance to share. Yes, indeed, I rise within from the sleeping memories of time. The years have gone by, and yet all is happening as you are present as now.

All consciousness' that have ever existed are with you as one. It is never ending, it is without beginning, and it is a place where you will finally rest.

All that you are and all that the universe and God has brought you is yours for eternities to share, to know, to remember. It is in the act of remembering that you bring some peace into your lifetime, now awakening from the time of the great forgetting, the time where everything else slips away between you and the Light of the divine within you. (H)

* * *

Parts of Consciousness

If one accepts that humans bring into this lifetime only fragments of past consciousness then the questions arise, "Where are the other fragments? Are there other humans, now alive, that have more pieces in their memories?" The answer that Mary gives us is, "Yes."

* * *

My lifetimes took very many changes and at this time, yes indeed, there are parts of my consciousness that are in physical form. As we spoke of the consciousness it can be shared by many. There is not one who is walking around as Miriam but I can gather now to me *that* consciousness and all those experiences that were known to me in my humanity and share them with you. (G)

* * *

No Coincidence

In this life we are surrounded by other people. To some we have a close connection, others not. Some we like instantly, and others we do not. Is there a reason that those in our life are near, and are they, at least in part, here for our spiritual growth? Again Mary answers with a, "Yes."

* * *

And those in your life are gathered to you with memories of not just that life but of others that were shared together. Many ask why so many from the Christed consciousness are gathering at this time. It is the time of Light, it is the time of transformation on your planet and in the universe, as it was then. Trust-even those here with doubt. Yes, you are gathering together again, yes you remember and you feel. You know those of you who listened with hearts opened wide, those who listened to the words and shook their heads in disbelief, those who were curious and listened and questioned and wondered. The one thing that you all hold now is that you have all been drawn here and your consciousness has raised, just as it did then. Are not many of you opening as workers of Light? Are not many of you being called and drawn to seek the vibration of Light, to seek the truth, to lift from the density of the humanity into that which is so much more? Yes, you walked with us. Yes, you remember. Yes, you practiced your faith and you were true to your faith as was I. For I was a good Jew. And so was Jesus. You will turn the head of many with that statement. But we looked then to shed the labels, to shed those boundaries that held us in corrals of belief, that held us in laws and rules being created by the humanity that we carried our light in. We were asked then to see the same Light of the Divine within each man, woman and child and we are being asked to see again. Welcome back. There is much work to do and so it will be done...and so it will be done! (G)

* * *

CHAPTER   TWO

Where Truth Can Be Found

"Trust with your heart, trust with your vision of what you have within you; of that magnificent Light that will illumnate truth before you, that will guide you ever homeward and on your way."

As you read this book you will have to decide what to believe. Our beliefs are truth to us. As children most of us were told what to believe by those adults around us. As we grow, if we question those beliefs, we may keep or modify some and discard others. In the spiritual realm, which is the core essence of this book, we can not prove any of it with our rational logical mind. In the end, we either believe what has entered our life or we do not, for free choice is always given to us. The realization of truth lies outside our logical minds, in an other conscious recognition. This recognition is the only way to really KNOW. Mary explains this way to know and also gives a short definition of blasphemy which is useful in our search for spiritual truth.

Denying Inner Truth

* * *

It is not blasphemous to question the interpretation of one man to another. It is only blasphemous to hear the word of God in your heart and deny it. To hear the truth of your soul and to ignore it and to not strive to love yourself as purely as you can; that is blasphemous. (C)

* * *

Just as Much Truth as Light

The process of editing has occurred throughout history. It was no different with manuscripts written about Jesus, his teachings, and his followers The result of editing is that we have truth and distortion, side by side, in the material we read.

Where Truth Can Be Found

* * *

There were those who would benefit by losing information. Has that changed even in this world in which you live? Is not information lost and found, distorted, to create a reality in the hands that hold it? Can not every man have the capacity to create "truth" through manipulation, through ego? Things have not changed. Things have also not changed that there is just as much Light as ever, just as much truth as ever. And many many more find their vision within and look through the eyes of that vision to what is being presented to them and ask, "Is this my truth.?" (C)

* * *

Writings Validate What We Know

* * *

It is good that you ask this. This is what I alluded to before and you heard so clearly. Our humanity, that which we had accepted to come into, to move about this planet, has a need for validations of the words that were spoken and the truth that we were taught. That which was written, know was written by the hand of humanity. Some of it very pure, some of it seen through the emotion of the one who wrote it.

That which is being channeled by the higher guardians and guides of Light, in essence, carries truth. Indeed much of it is the same truth. Some of the guardians of Light, if they came from humanity and have now transcended into Light sometimes carry some of the same slanted views of things. For all that is in Light does not necessarily hold all the truths. Only that part that vibrates in the frequency of pure universal consciousness. (F)

* * *

Having Knowledge and Wisdom

***

Passing the knowledge, I believe, Gnostic was given title, meaning knowledge.   So the knowledge was passed, some took it, some didn't. It was difficult for those to remember that each one of us were vessels of Light, that was the main teachings of those writings - keepers of Light, of truth, all having access to the greater knowledge, to the greater visions.   There were those leaders who knew that and yet just believed that only those in power had access to that knowledge and to the visions. It was a very difficult thing for them to accept that each and every man and woman could have vision, understanding of truth, and so it will be again. There will be confusion, there will be denial and there will be those that accept, once again, the Light within themselves. (C)

***

Jesus' Truth Not Always Accepted

Truth goes beyond the conscious mind - there is a resonance in other parts of one's being, especially in the heart, that tells us what is true.   Perhaps, in our humanity, we can never know total truth,   because it changes as we grow and evolve.

***

I listened as you spoke and in truth we are always listening, waiting, for those of you to reach for us.   Many of those of Light stand with their love and with their hearts open. Indeed, you do remember the

Where Truth Can Be Found

sitting at his side. It is not the first time I have spoken of sitting by him, the man called Jesus, Yesuha to us. The peace, the joy, sometimes the confusion, because not all that was spoken to us was understood at first and I dare not give you the idea that every word that fell from his lips was taken by us as drops of rain in the soil. Even though we questioned, we knew there was truth. We could feel it and you could sense it in his eyes, in his heart, in his touch, even in the sound of his voice we knew that there was something being spoken that was not merely of humanity. It was beyond the limits of what we knew and yet there was a difference.

All of us had studied in the laws of Abraham and the rules of Moses and the great prophets before. The men studied more formally, the women catching bits and pieces like crumbs falling from the table and yet what he spoke rang out in truth even though some things were so different. I enjoyed the fact that it was different because what was taught to us I questioned. The others who followed did not question the truth of their own faith but were looking for more, were yearning for more, desiring more. And more he had and more he gave. Not profound words, he was not an eloquent speaker, simple truths, many times asking us to gaze at things as if we were seeing them for the first time. He used very little words, but somehow we felt what it was that was being said. More was said in the stillness of his presence and love than was ever said in speech, in lecture. In teaching, I spoke once how the children sat and listened to him, how they were drawn to him, how they hung on each word, waiting for the next word to fall. The adults were not different, we would do very much the same only very many times he would say, "Share with me what you are thinking." "Tell me what you are feeling now, what is your truth, what do you know of God and of yourself?" I don't think I was ever asked that in all of my years, "What do I think of God?" "What is my truth?" My truth was what I was taught - what I was led to believe. It was not mine, it was the laws as they were written. It was the word of the great teachers as they were handed down. And he asks me now, "What is my truth?" Oh, did he get answers! Much to his dismay also. Answers did not fall that easily from the learned ones.

It was the men who had studied. The men who had more of a knowledge of the laws of God than any of the women and yet they had less understanding of themselves. They would grasp at words looking for the right things to say trying to make sense where there was none. He would never judge but rather sit and with that smile, with that look, there was no judgement - an understanding though. There was something about his gaze that when you were confused, if you caught his eyes, the veil lifted, the walls came down and there was no more confusion. He somehow was able to bring you to your heart rather than your mind - pure soul - pure spirit. To the Light that he taught was within us and in that Light things were so much clearer. Indeed, in Light, all things are clearer.

We struggle so to learn, to understand the ways of God, to understand the mysteries of the universe and yet, sitting in our Light without words, all is answered. Maybe difficult to explain to another, but isn't your truth to be your own and isn't the greatest gift you can give but to lead somebody to find their truth? Much preparation for his life was made by many groups. The Essenes knew that he would be coming. Other prophets, unknown to you, names that you will not find in your writings, also knew of the message that would be brought. It was an understanding that they were seeking and those that looked for that found it. Those that looked for the glory and power of God to use it in this world and did not find it were disillusioned in their crossing over. In their beginning into Light they were not disillusioned anymore. The answers waited for them. Perhaps they struggled through their humanity a little harder than those who had found the way but is that not so even now.

As we gaze from Light, at humanity now, we see the struggle, and we see the road much easier traveled when the Light and the peace of the word of God is within you. Use this and be at peace with yourselves. Your journey will be simpler and you can spend more time enjoying what is around you, the people, the feelings, all the beauty of all the living things that have been provided for you. Question not the Light of God and behold the beauty of all that there is. This is the message I bring to you now. (I)

* * *

Go Within for Truth

Mary of Bethany also speaks of the trouble Jesus found himself in when he challenged traditional religious authority.

* * *

He had a lot of nerve to tell his students to go within, that all they needed to grow was to go within and to find their own power and find their own God within instead of looking *without* to the Pharisees and the Saducees. He did not disagree with all of the formalities, that is not what he was against. He was against abuses by people that set themselves up to play God when they weren't God, when they were only human.

* * *

Inner Truth without Judgement

The line between discernment and judgement is often not clear, whether pertaining to people or ideas. Magdalene asks us to set aside self-judgment when we are searching for our truths.

* * *

Trust with your heart, trust with your vision of what you have within you, of that magnificent Light that will illuminate truth before you, that will guide you ever homeward and on your way. It is difficult to remain in spirit while in humanity but this is your greatest gift. Connecting to your spirit and living it through your humanity is a gift that has been given. Is it not the gift that Yesuha, Buddha, Mohammed and many others tried to bring into Light? You need not step aside your body and your mind but honor them. How else will you interpret your visions if not through the mind that was given you?

Falling from spirit is what you allude to, many fearing that they fall out of the grace of God when they despair, when they experience their humanity. This is the time to cherish and honor the spirit within. It is the time that draws us to spirit and should not draw us away from it. It is the time for reaching, for not falling away from, for in spirit there is comfort. That which you feel to be your shortcomings are just steps along the way. Be without judgement. The words he spoke so many times, "Be without judgement of self." This is where it begins. (C)

* * *

Heart Truth is Increasing

Mary tells us something very encouraging about our time; that consciousness and human heart energy or awareness is increasing. As this is occurring, so is our capacity to know truth.

* * *

What I bring to you you know to be truth in your heart and need only to hear the words spoken, as I will speak them to you. It is a time in your universe of great awakening - this is not new to you. This message is heard over and over, it comes from many, it comes from those who speak from what you call the "other side" and those who speak because they have heard it and repeat only, not knowing if it is truth.

The vibration of your planet is rising. It is a time of great excitement for many. Indeed, the veil is growing thinner and it is your choice to listen to the words of your heart, to listen to Light as it resonates within you or your choice to turn a deaf ear and not hear it all except the ramblings of your mind. Know what thoughts are mere illusions and what is your truth. Your truth will not come from the noise that

constantly goes over and over in your mind the way
the otter plays in the water, repeating the same
action time and time again mindlessly and effortlessly.   It is time to know what is important for your
humanity and what is important for your experience,
for you to feel. (J)

* * *

CHAPTER   THREE

Reincarnation
Death - Transition

"A part of our conscious-
ness will return when it is called
upon but our presence, our existence, remains ever connected to
the Light, to the One."

As you read this book with an open mind you may con-
sider that reincarnation is part of life eternal.   A channeled
spirit, such as the Magdalene, is demonstrating to us that the
life force does not extinguish when the physical body that
houses that spirit can no longer continue. Reincarnation has
many variables and therefore one word can not describe all the
various beliefs. Mary Magdalene, who has had the experience
of being both on earth and elsewhere in spirit, gives us much to
think about on this subject.

All Souls of One Inseparable Energy

* * *

You are confused and yet very close to holding
the truth.   But then again you always were.   In the
Love and Light of God we are all of one energy, inseparable, each part shining brightly with one another.   As
you step forward into humanity, and not to confuse you
all, but as you step forth into many shapes and forms
(not only humanity as you know it on this earth), each
time you move forth with the memories, with the consciousness of all you have experienced before you.

You speak of past lives as if they could be num-
bered one to twelve.   As endless as time that is how
many lifetimes and experiences you may have had.
"Old souls." I have heard it said, and we have referred
to it.   But before myself and other guides, no soul is
older than another. We are all from the beginning and
all from the Light of God. Old souls are just those who
tend to remember more of where they have been and
feel very "old" and burdened by all their lifetimes, but
in reality can not possibly remember all.

As you transition and move into the Light of your consciousness, your awareness, the Light and Love that you are will expand in and join with the others. All is shared. No guide is more powerful than another, no being of Light any stronger or any brighter. All is as one. All is shared as one.

When a spark of divine, a being of Light, chooses to come into form and for your understanding the form of humanity, you come with those memories of lifetimes that were shared not only by you but by others. You take into each life that which you choose to explore, that which you choose to experience.

Indeed, part of the woman named Judith in this lifetime has brought forth in this lifetime the consciousness and awareness of me. I have chosen this vehicle to speak. She has chosen to remember, she has allowed herself to step into those memories that we share. It is not all that she is and it is not all that I am. What she brings forward in me is a connection to all that I saw, that I experienced, that I felt as I walked with the man named Jesus. It was not the only lifetime that I had and this is not the only lifetime I experience now.

Indeed each one of you holds the awareness, the consciousness, before you. What draws you together is that which you carry that recognizes one another. Those that carry the conscious awareness, the truths and experiences of that time, in your universe are drawn together so that you may remember.

You can choose to trust this and to move into

that space of your mind and as you do you may open up to all the memories as she has. Yes, I rise within her as she drinks from what I have to offer, as she allows that to flow through her as I freely share all that I know, all that I have seen and all that I have felt. (I)

* * *

Reincarnation - Your Choice

Those who embrace the idea of reincarnation may wonder if returning involves free choice.

* * *

Many debate returning to physical form again and again, what is referred to as reincarnation. If we are to look at some of the words that have been written correctly, references were made of the return to humanity again and again, if that be your choice. (G)

* * *

Past Life Followers of Jesus

As spiritual seekers continue their journey in this life, many experience memories of past lives This, according to Mary, is as it should be. Usually these memories are incomplete which, when one thinks about it, is no different than memories in our present lifetime.

* * *

Humanity wants the answers to be brought to them. When it is time to remember, it will come and be known to you. Your name already is in your heart and in your mind. Each one of your souls has memories of the journeys you have taken. Each one of your souls has that which holds the visions of "the one" who has walked before. Upon death, you join the Light of God and you join the memories of all.

When you come into this humanity you bring with you many of those thoughts, many of those visions, many of those words. You have chosen to bring them forward in this lifetime to understand humanity in a different way. Indeed, many sitting before me know that their connection to Yeshua was more than what they were taught as a child. Many have memories; it stirs within them eagerly, dismissed by the conscious mind - "This can not possibly be true." For those of you who have memories, that feel and somehow know that you stood before him and felt his smile and his eyes and his touch and his love; is it not doubt and unworthiness that does not allow that door to swing open for you to step in? Look into your heart and see which doors are closed - begin - begin to look now. Begin to feel what it is you already know. (J)

* * *

Precarnation - Jesus and Others

According to Mary, before we come to live in humanity, we know, in spirit, the purpose for that life.

* * *

Long before we came into physical being Yeshua and myself and the others knew what our journey would entail. (C)

Rest your heart. He touched many of us with his life, with his physical presence and with his love. There is no ending; our souls return many times to learn and grow and to experience this world, to understand what he came to understand and to bring Light to others around us. Those who have been called to us were with him then. You have him in your heart, there is nothing to fear. Embrace him, call upon your heart to call to you the truth.

Open your mind and heart and you will know your place at his side. There is nothing to feel guilty about. Being able to touch upon a man as great and as loving as he that remembered God's Light and helped you to remember it also. Be at peace with it. (B)

* * *

Many Lifetimes

Mary was asked about her journey through human lifetimes.

* * *

Yes, I have had some lifetimes and there are some that have been shared and one that was shared with part of your consciousness. There is a sense and feeling of knowing. My lifetimes took very many changes and at this time, yes indeed, there are parts of my consciousness that are in physical form. As we spoke, the consciousness can be shared by many. There is not one who is walking around as Miriam but I can gather now to me that consciousness and all those experiences that were known to me in my humanity and share them with you.

Many of my lifetimes were not ones of great importance. Humanity looks for those famous names. However, I did sit in the court of a king of England!

That part of my consciousness had *quite* an experience and even in that, the purpose was to bring Light and awareness of the Divine. It was not received well, and yes, parts of my consciousness of what you call my soul, experienced a lifetime in which I walked on the side of darker and heavier energy, thought and human response. I have learned much and I hope to continue to share as so many do, what we have learned and what we know to be truth. If you want a number, in this lifetime, my consciousness is in that of five mortal beings. Enough is said. (G)

* * *

Known in Other Lifetimes

A woman asks, "Mary I sense we may have known each other in another time and I was wondering if that is true and if you could tell me how we might have known each other then?"

* * *

Yes, we did. A part of my consciousness and of yours shared a life, a life you may or may not remember. It was a life on the continent known as Africa. In that lifetime we worked as healers. I was a male energy at that time. The male energy was allowed to be dominant, yours female. Much of what we did was in making remedies, healings, using that which grew from the ground, that which you refer to as shamanic in your culture. We worked with that which grew and we worked with spirit. It was unusual in tribes at that time for a man and woman to walk the same path and yet we did.

It was in my consciousness at that time that did

what the Christed energy taught me and I embraced a female as an equal in my healings and together we worked side by side, again much to the dismay of many.

* * *

"Thank you Mary. Will I be using some of that knowledge in this lifetime as I open to become a healer using the spirit and other modalities?"

* * *

Yes, you will. I will give you a small insight. Listen to the sounds of drums. Allow the music, the vibration of drumming to guide you to your passage of memory as healer to awaken that part that you can then bring forward into this lifetime in a way that can be used for the highest good of many. (G)

* * *

Mary is asked again about other shared lifetimes.

* * *

More than one lifetime. Bethany is laughing, she says that you have known her also in many lifetimes. It seems that we managed to become entangled in the most curious ways. There were a few of us that trip and fall over one another before we know and see who we are.

There was a time when we gave up much. Celibate and pious, believing that this was the way. I dare say we cast off the cloth and had lifetimes that ran for the hills for the chastising that we took. We had to take different names and still we taught his word, taught it with children growing inside of us, allowing seeds to be planted. Instead of sacrifice, we opened to the abundance of the universe, an abundance of experiences. We moved in Light many times in many ways. The time of the cloth, I dare say, you left before me. And as I left my body, you wore the cloth to welcome me. It was not of our humanity that we made light but rejoiced in being allowed to experience it at all.

The greatest gift is to be in the flesh, to feel in the flesh, to cry and to laugh in the flesh. This is why we keep doing it and why we will continue. I dare say your lifetimes are not over - we will meet again. (M)

* * *

Remembering Life Lessons

There are those who wonder why we would want to reincanate, and why we place so much importance on our humanity when some lives appear to be filled with pain and deprivation.

A woman in the audience asks, "After humans leave this life do they become enlightened and experience a realization of what their lives were about, what their effect was on other people?

* * *

I thank you for the questions you asked for they lie in the heart of all. To be in humanity, to be in physical is to wonder about the time when this will no longer exist, as we know it, as you see it now. For many there is fear and wonder, for some, in sadness I must say, there are thoughts of escaping that which you dwell in to go into another place, to leave what seems to be so difficult, to go into what seems to be so much easier. I must speak of this. To transcend into Light is not easier than to be in the form that you sit in now. Yes, you will be different there. Yes, the vibration, the energy, the consciousness changes shape and appearance. Yes, it expands into places beyond what you can see and touch and taste. But these are senses that you hold so dearly to you now or sometimes not so dearly at all, and sometimes you wish to discard.

The truth that you wish to resolve, to understand, you can do in the body before me and in the now by moving into those places of consciousness, by following the path of Light, by believing that you are indeed Abba and Abba indeed is you, for if you do not believe it now you will not believe it when your body disintegrates before you. That which you take as truth, you take with you and there are indeed different levels of understanding even after what you perceive to be death.

Indeed, everything changes as you look at it now but in consciousness nothing changes at all. If you do not seek truth now, you will not seek truth then, even when it is laid before you. The greatest of all understandings can be placed before you and you will be blind to it. Yes, you have access to all wisdom, to all knowing, when you transcend into Light. You also have the free will and the freedom to turn, to not embrace, to not raise as high as you can, to not accept all that you are. For some this is beyond comprehension. It is not punishment when you transcend into Light and do not open to all that is possible to you. It is your choice.

Yeshua came into the human form, into humanity for many reasons. He spoke from flesh so that you could embrace from flesh all the endless possibilities. You were to embrace from flesh that you could be as he was, that you could believe as he did, that you could see what he saw, that you could heal as he healed: to know that you were sons and daughters of God and brothers and sisters in Light. You chose then as you choose now and will continue to choose how far that you will allow the consciousness of the Light within you to reach beyond that which you can see and bring into your heart now the greatest peace and joy. A joy as great as any being of Light, as great as any archangel and any prophet. It is yours; it will always be yours.

The message is for you now. Yes, you hear and yes, you see, and yes, the consciousness continues and can speak to those in humanity now. You can help to heal what was not healed in this flesh by many. You can communicate to those that are not in form now and together both you and that which you cannot see or barely see, can come to greater Light and awareness. This is possible. Choose wisely. (L)

* * *

No Pain in Death

To come again means, of course, that one has to leave, to transition, to die. As Mary has already said, we, in humanity, usually view death with wonder and fear. She tells us more about the leaving and the transition.

* * *

At the time of letting go of all that you know, understand; there is no pain. The pain is the hanging on, the holding on to that which does not serve you in your physical life as well as in your spiritual one. Recognize the Light within your own soul and you will understand that Light to which you will return. (A)

* * *

After Life

Dr. Bezmen asks, "Mary, in the afterlife you seem very at peace. Will we meet our guide and what is there when we go on?"

* * *

As you cross over there is a time of reflection Time has no measure. The past is now, as is the future. The reflection is that which has passed and the lessons that have been learned and gifts are taken from this time. Then there is a return to the One, to the source of all as the spark of Light journeys ever homeward. Parts of the consciousness remain; we do not linger in your worldly place. A part of our consciousness will return when it is called upon but our presence, our existence remains ever connected to the Light, to the One. Our enlightened peace is eternal; it is more beautiful than can be described. It has no form It is a loving, a loving that has not words. I struggle for words. Loving is so misunderstood. It is all that there is. It is connecting to that feeling that you feel in your heart and in your soul as you gaze upon a newborn baby or as you look with compassion and it fills every cell of your existence.

A part of our consciousness can choose to experience other lessons or we can choose to stay as just consciousness, as Light. Our connection to the One stays in our soul as it stays within you. The Light that is the spark of your life is the breath that you take. It is all that there is as you cross. As you make that change you will be greeted by all those who have walked with you, all consciousness becomes as one, there is no judgement as we have been led to believe by some of those who lead us with good intention. There is only understanding. There is only love and wisdom and there is only peace. Our only discomfort is in seeing the unrest in those that we love and leave behind. (A)

* * *

Death in Dreams

Some of us have dreams of death and communi-cating with those who are no longer in physical form. Mary tells us the purpose of this when a woman asks, "What does it mean when you dream about the deceased? "

* * *

There is much fear of the unknown, even those of great faith doubt of the existence of life that never ends. Many of those who have passed on, try with love and with Light to guide and direct us. It is the fear of hearing them, of sensing them, of seeing them that holds us back. Dream is a safe place. It is a place that they may come, they may speak to you, they may show you their presence without arousing the doubt and fear of your human condition. For when you dream you are not of physical self but that of spirit at a deeper consciousness. Even in the messages of those dreams that are perceived to be bad there are messages and lessons to be learned. Sometimes those negative dreams are telling you to confront your fears, showing you your fears and then allowing you to awaken and realize that you can walk through fear and not dissolve in it. That you can open your eyes and continue to breath as we pass through our greatest tasks, our deepest fears, our most terrible sorrows. One feels as though the next breath will not come. It does! Dream allows that. In the quiet of the night they speak to you. You may listen to them safely there.

Do not take anything as bad. Sometimes it is the symbol; sometimes it is to give you strength. Send Light to those who come to you. If you are not sure of their intent merely send them your Light from your heart and look into their eyes. When you see in the eyes the love and the Light, then draw them closer to you. If you see anything that does not feel of Light, push it away and know that it is a test, a lesson. One will come to you this evening. She has tried many times. She will speak of something that will surprise you - I allow her her space. (A)

* * *

CHAPTER   FOUR

Mary Magdalene - - "Miriam"

"I was a bit more brazen than some women, this I will take responsibility for, a little outspoken perhaps but he, (Jesus), gave me the courage to speak what was in my heart."

Since this information was delivered by the energy of Mary Magdalene there was much questioning from those who heard her words about her background and relationship to Jesus. The New Testament writers speak of her but with little detail. The fact that her name is even known after 2000 years is remarkable and indicates her importance as would the tip of an iceberg. The reader needs to consider two ideas. First, at that time women had less worth than livestock and, except in unusual circumstances, no power. Second, the men that followed Jesus were members of a society that devalued women. There is scriptural evidence that some of those men were not pleased that Jesus not only considered Mary an equal but a special confidant. The devaluing of women continued when a group of men decided which writings would be considered "Holy" and which would be left out of the Bible. Finally, a pope decided to make Mary a prostitute to justify her presence in scripture.

Who was this woman that she had such a special place in the life of Jesus and the community that formed around his teaching? Why is her spirit energy returning at this time?

Magdalene's Soul Purpose

* * *

I have been with you; my arrival is not new. I spent a lot of my time nurturing and loving. There are many that are in need. Everyone that I see before me as I channel, as I go from soul to soul, is seeking love and seeking peace. It is that seeking of love and peace that draws me, for in my lifetime I sought the same. I was not of poverty as some proclaim, I had much that was material and then I saw him.

He passed through my village, he and a group. There was so much peace and yet so much fear. His eyes were of love and his heart was open and I followed. I follow those whose hearts are open who call for help. When the quiet of the night feels despair, I know of despair. I know of grief and loss but I also know of love and of healing.

What you refer to as miracles are gifts of the heart, beautiful hearts, so filled with love. This healing can happen again, it has happened lifetime through lifetime. I just come and gently guide those who may need somebody who is, what you may refer to as, more real, more human. I am not of the angelic realm, merely mortal who has passed and continues because there is no end and there is so much beauty. So much love, yet we look to the pain and to the loss of things that can not be retrieved. We clutch to what we do not have instead of embracing what lies so close. I embrace all that there is and extend hands to those who need guidance to remember, to remember that there is no end and to remember what lies around them. The very breath that I feel in this body is a testament to life and must be honored.

There are those who seek answers. Look into your heart, listen quietly, there are misgivings, there are misunderstandings, there are misinterpretations, all that could be honored is what you know to be truth. The other guides speak of universal awakening. It begins in each heart, as does a ripple when a pebble is tossed into water. It will not be in this lifetime that all will change but mark, each one will see that change as they cross into a different aspect of self. They will miss nothing as they have missed nothing in the past. They will see all and know all and find peace even in the darkest moment. You call on spirits of Light. I know of nothing, I have seen nothing that does not contain Light within. (A)

* * *

Personal History

* * *

I was a *bit* older than Mary of Bethany at the time that I met the Christ, the one they call the Son of God. I was raised in a small sea town, my father was of wealth and I was well educated within our home. I was sent to a schooling unknown to most people where I was taught the ways of the goddess.

* * *

Dr. Bezmen asks, "Where was that school, Mary?"

* * *

The school resided in what you refer to as Egypt. Many were sent there, a lot of young women like myself, as girls. We were taught the ways of the goddess and instructed on caring for other people. And when we were of age, we were retrieved by our parents and given in marriage. I was given in marriage to a man quite a few years older than myself. It was arranged. The marriage was not one of great happiness. I separated myself from him and made my way, returning back to my village, and doing what needed to be done to survive. It was at a small village as I stood by a well that I listened to Yesh speak to the children and women of things I had never heard before. I was drawn to him and that is where it began.

* * *

Dr. Bezmen asks, "You mention the name "Yesh". Is that what you called Yeshua?"

* * *

That is the most understandable of the expressions that I can give you now - there were many names.

* * *

Dr. Bezmen asks, "Can you remember what he was first teaching when you heard him?"

* * *

He was telling the children about a flower he held in his hand. He was showing the roots of the flower from the earth and how they would go deep into the ground to be held fast and how its leaves and its flower reached to the sun for its Light. And he spoke of us as being flowers on this earth reaching to the Light of God. There were many women around him with the children. I never saw a Rabbi with women in his company, it was most unusual. Jesus was a teacher. He studied well and he taught with his heart.

* * *

Dr. Bezmen asks, "So how did you get to follow him after hearing him at the well? How did that come about?"

* * *

It was difficult for me at the time. There was so much I was afraid of, so much I didn't understand. It was foreign to me, the God he spoke of. It did not fit into what I had been taught or into what had been taught to those around me. I approached him slowly. He caught my eye and reached for my hand and I knew at once that I had come home and that there was much I was to learn. He gave me, his self, his understanding and I in return gave him my duties, my money and followed him as student and as teacher. (B)

* * *

Mary and Other Followers

Dr. Bezmen asks, "Could you tell us the year that you were born in a way that we would understand it now?

* * *

It is not difficult although many time frames throughout history have altered. It is a perspective for the easiest understanding of those who seek such information. I was born twelve years prior to the birth of the man named Jesus, the man who we called Yeshua, the man who we followed. The man who embraced us all, the man who would call us his gathering, his family, his points of Light in a darkened world.

Yes, I was older than he. In many of those years there was much seeking of my soul, much longing for answers of all that there is, of the wonders of the universe. There have been times when we have spoken of the early years. I was referred to very often only by those practices of Hebrew faith, the faith that is written, that is looked at, that is studied. But in my time and the time of my ancestors there were many studies of spirit, there were many schools of thought as there are now. The younger years were spent in the study of the goddess, of the earth, of all living things and their connection. Different than what is studied and spoken of now. It was more an understanding of all. That we are in spirit of all the gifts that we possess, of all the parts of ourselves, like holding a beautiful clear stone to the sun. The studies of the goddess taught me methods of healing, the laying of herbs, the anointing of oils, the fragrances, the awakening of all the senses of humanity and understanding the greater connection. It was of spirit, of earth; it was of the seen and the unseen. It was of pleasure and of pain, it was of all that you can imagine and that can encompass the mind.

In the town where I was born there were those who practiced the ways of the goddess and those that were of the Hebrew faith. I knew of both. There were no clear lines between the two, much crossed over in those days as they do now by the women. It is not unlike your practice now, so many revering the mother, Mary, the mother of Yeshua. And in our faith there was reverence of many of the females that walked before us in spirit and in strength identifying with that part of ourselves that was woman, that was goddess and essence. To understand the divine is to understand all aspects of both man and woman. So in those days my studies were deep and rich in many faiths, in many beliefs, in many paths. (I)

I have spoken of my travels, I have spoken even of my marriages and no they were not to the man named Yeshua.   Great disappointment to scholars, I know, but I was not his wife although I was a wife of one that I would rather forget.   Arranged, yes, part of me went along with the arrangement.   I knew that there was something to learn but as I broke free and sought out a greater truth I found him.   The whispers went among all the town's people that Yeshua was coming, the one with the crazy ideas, the one who embraced women, the one who said we could drop our veils.   It was blasphemous and it delighted me.

I could not wait to see a man, a rabbi it was said, who said to drop the veil and to speak, to step forward, that he wished to hear our thoughts of God. Not that I was a skeptic but I did stand behind and watch and listen to his words.   In the town there was a great well, a gathering place in most of our towns, a place to draw water, to gather people to share stories. It was a place where women gathered to talk of their children and their men, to talk in secret of their beliefs, of their practices of their rituals.

It was also there where the men gathered, after the women left, to speak of the fields and to speak of the matter of taxes, of government, of the rabbis and those in power.   They would discuss what they would say and what was the new word and who we were to follow.

It was there that I heard him, men, women and children gathering, at first slowly, some more boldly challenging him standing with their hands crossed, especially the men.   Who was this Yeshua to defy the laws of Abraham, who was he to openly touch women, even in their unclean time?   Such a smile and yet something deeper within him. You might call it defiance.   He was not a stupid man.   He knew it would raise eyebrows. He knew the path that he was taking and did not seem to hold any caution to his tongue. Even I would grimace at times at his outspokenness.   I drew closer and closer and my heart opened and my mind and all that I was and could be.   I could be as gifted as the goddesses; I could feel my humanity, experience my senses and pleasures. I could know and feel the loving power of God. I know that the man that I stood beside was an equal to me, no different, except in appearance.   It was a delight and a joy and a freedom to be able to talk of the stars, to be able to talk openly of Moses and faith. To be able to speak of the laying on of hands and the raising of the dead. Elijah! And how could this be?   What seemed at one time stars of my people now became a reality. When I could touch words I could hear and feel that what I dreamed of was right before my eyes. The Light in others and those that backed away, those that covered their faces as not to be seen as one who would listen to him because what if rabbi were to hear? What if the elders were to know that we listened to Yeshua's rantings? "Stop looking outside and around yourself - look into your heart - know your own roots - and follow them into the earth for they are those that sustain you. Look to the stars for they speak to you - look to the Light of God inside of you. Do not pay honor to me or to any other rabbi - do not hold in more esteem than thyself.   Do not hold government in greater power than thyself."   Outspoken he was.   Eyebrows were raised but the teachings and the words went on. I had a bit of wealth behind me. It helped sustain he and the others.

They speak of the twelve around him but there were many more. The twelve were seen by so many as the twelve tribes coming together. A symbol of what he was to do and in truth he was to unite our hearts - to help us all see the sameness in each other. To feel the presence of God equally within each other. He was not to be a king or a leader but he could not denounce the fact that prophet would be labeled on him and prophet he would wear. John the Baptist was mentor for him. Many times they spoke, many times they planned together. Many times they saw the same visions of their people. They took their own paths but Yeshua was to do so much more the laying on of hands. Jesus was not the only healer to do this.

There were endless days and nights of embracing each other, the newness, the freedom to touch. Men and women no longer fearing to brush against each others skin, yet occasionally still looking around to see who would notice. The comfort we found, the healing that grew, the strength of a nation of people that were to be as one, one beautiful Light and hope. As you know, things did not go exactly as planned for on your earth and in your world there is not a oneness, at least not that is seen at this time but it is rising, rising from the depths of each heart.

More are seeking to journey as I did, perhaps not on foot but in their minds, looking for One Truth, One Light that could surround and hold and embrace

Mary Magdalene - Miriam

all that we are. It is rising. Twelve tribes are now twelve hundred, twelve thousand, twelve million. There is still One Light. Numbers have changed and grown but truth can not be changed, *(The Magdalene pauses)*, Drawing near, perhaps Yeshua has entered this space. His presence is here. He comes with full heart. He comes with many blessings for the hearts of all. His words are spoken by so many in so many ways.

Let it be known at this time that it is in his message of Light that each one comes to their truth, they come to the place that he had found. Your life need not be lost but you may face the same obstacles that he did. Those that would separate you, those that would challenge your beliefs, those that would beckon you to follow their way, their truth, their rules, their laws. But your hearts are stronger and your Lights are brighter as many are, and you are finding comfort from deep within you. That is what we felt with him, that is what we taught after his passing. To be comfortable in your own presence, your truth is your truth and it will fill you with delight and joy, it will radiate from your heart and from your eyes, from your words. No longer mattering who heard, who agrees, who disagrees, who follows, who doesn't. Your path is your own as his path was his own and we could not convince him to turn back, to be still and to be quiet, to hold his tongue. You are to walk your truth when you find it. Let it be food as it is said for your soul. Let the Light of the universe of God fill you so completely that you no longer hunger and thirst but you can take it from that place inside. It does not mean you are to take to the hills and fast, though that can bring you to that place inside rather quickly, but it is not necessary.

Be still in your heart, feel and begin to remember the part of self that knew his words for all on this earth were there then, some with more memory and some with less.   Some with connection and some without, some who will see and some who will cover their eyes as we covered our faces with veils.   Some who will speak of it and some who will not dare say a word of remembering.   Remember even a glimpse of rabbi, of Yeshua, of his dream of us being as one and not of being still another separate religion.   Of embracing each other, in all of our likenesses, to dare to believe in what we can not see.   The gifts that dwell in our hearts, the healing that comes only when we can reach and touch another.   Do we not shrivel and die for lack of touch?   So can we not heal and replenish and restore with the same?   Such simple things he would ask of us always a question for a question.   An answer that came effortlessly and then another one would come.

There were sleepless nights, endless days of difficulties yes, and joys.   There was anger and frustration, even a sense of betrayal and loss.   He would have us feel it all and so many did.   I ask you in your hearts to find that Light: it is there.   And if he stood before you in flesh one glance and it would ignite like an oil lamp in the darkness.   It would rise like the seas and fall with the tides.   One look and you knew what truth was - it was you - it was universe - it was God - it was goddess.   It was compassion.   It was the sound of children running and laughing and playing, it was the sound of men arguing and women gossiping.   It was all and is all and it is laid before you as he

Mary Magdalene - Miriam

taught us - do not hide from life - do not hide from tears - do not hide from laughter - do not hide what you can give so freely to others: do not hide from what others can give so freely to you.

His greatest message, his greatest teaching was to walk one foot before the other, to feel the earth, to know the goodness, to offer comfort to one another, to be a strength to one another. To be patient with self and one another, to be one tribe, one tribe of humanity and spirit to be as one Light and one truth. The Light is being passed now through so many, can you reach for it, can you take it as your own and live one truth as one people? This we pray for you and we walk with you and guide you and protect you, but only if you receive it. And so be his word that continues and will always be. Take it or allow it to pass through you and take what you need from it. You cannot fail in his eyes. (N)

* * *

Mary Observes Jesus Teaching

* * *

I first laid my eyes on him talking and playing with children. How often I saw him arms open wide, heart open, eyes burning with a Light and a Love that there are no words for, the love and the comfort that fills you from within, that rises within your heart and soul and burst forth bringing tears to your eyes of joy, of comfort. Yes, indeed he knew his connection to God, to the universe and to every man, woman and child that walked. This was the message he brought and oh how I was changed. He would sit and shake his head as we went from town to town, hamlet to hamlet, and he would hear of this man who came who was "God" on earth. A gentle smile he would get and said if they would only know the God within them all. It was a burden at times, how to bring the truth without bringing disillusionment to those who sought salvation and understanding not so much different than now. They would come seeking one that would come and save them all when all that they had within them was their salvation.

He spoke before the children. The children knew, they did not question the love that they felt. Hearts and eyes wide open, "Who is this man who comes and sits among us? It is as though he were our family. When strangers travel from afar they don't come into town feeling so at ease. Didn't he know his place? He was in our town." They would taunt him. They would challenge him. A man who would sit and smile that smile of delight. Everything they did he seemed to absorb as the sands would absorb the rain, drinking in their every action and word and finding delight in their questioning - never defensive - never self righteous - just comfort in knowing the word that he had and the message he had.

I followed him and so did many others. There were more than twelve. Many followed: we prepared meals together, we sang, we danced, we shared our stories, our thoughts of life of the universe of the stars above us. And he would sit and within one or two words bring a clarity to those questions. It wasn't how many words he spoke; it was what we felt in each word that was spoken. All made sense. We learned to hear with our hearts, not our heads or our ears but listening with senses that rose so deeply and knew the truth. (D)

I speak the words as Yeshua, yes, indeed we walked together - many of us walked together as many of us walk together now - knowing the truth - hearing that sound - feeling it stirring within.   Things around you not making sense yet great sense rising from the unseen.   The first time I laid eyes on him I stood back in the quiet shadows and listened to this man speak without effort, words that seemed to not be thought. You could look into his eyes and see the words coming from his eyes as they came from his lips. They poured from his heart, his words poured from his hands, a mere gesture brought a feeling of love and peace and comfort. A mere glance sent your heart racing home, the home you sought, the home you were looking to create and build and there it was in his words - there it was in his smile.   There was no rehearsed speech. Nothing could be rehearsed the way it fell from him as the waters fell from the springs.   They seemed to bubble up and pour out like liquid Light. They would bath you; the words wouldn't even enter your ears.   They somehow surrounded you and they held you as though he was holding you in the palms of his hands.

Many called him sorcerer.   Many accused and condemned what he was doing.   "Was this a spell he was casting on unsuspecting people?   Surely it had to be the work of something mysterious."   Those who spoke those words had never felt love, not this love, not this wholeness, not this beauty, nor this joy.

He was a man as we were all men and women. He embraced his humanity and asked us all to do the same, to not resent it or discard it or to turn from it or to hide from it, but to embrace it.   Every moment, every feeling, every joy, and you knew that this was the purpose of our humanity.   And to know that the God Light within you would be with you on your journey, that you did not do this alone, that you were not abandoned by God.

There was a little misunderstanding in the faith of my people.   You see, before he walked with us many of us, our fathers and the great prophets began to move from the core of truth, began to move deeper into their humanity and further and further away from the spirit that they knew that they were.   They began to separate themselves from the love and Light of God.   He and many have come to bring that truth into this journey.   That the God that you seek, that the comfort you seek is in your breath, is in your heart and is in each one of us.   It is truth as I hear, spoken before by this man who is present here; that there was a belief that it was only the men who were privy to this information.   It was taught by Abraham, it was taught by many, that there were roles of men and women clear and distinct.   As that separation grew wider so the separation of humanity and spirit grew wider.   For every time we find difference in one another we separate from the Light of God.

Those who feared him most were those who were walking the path that they were taught.   Many of the disciples questioned him, "Rabbi, the teachings, the teachings are not what we believe.   You have women sitting at your feet listening, and you speaking to them in public, not betrothed to them.   Are we not in defiance to the Law of God?"   He would smile and merely say, "No, but you are in defiance of the law of men.   Which do you follow, which do you choose?   Do you choose to follow the laws of God?   Do you wish to choose to follow the laws of your own heart and your own truth, or the ramblings of men, who detach themselves, who stand on the other side of the great abyss placing God on the top of the mountain and standing beneath it."

We would sit for hours and speak with him and he would ask us to listen with our hearts; to be still and quiet.   Many times he would not speak at all but ask us to merely feel the presence of God within us - to see it in the eyes of our children - to feel it in their breath as they slept.   Indeed this was different than what we had heard but this is what we longed for. This stirred us inside.   I was a bit more brazen than some women, this I will take responsibility for, a little outspoken perhaps but he gave me the courage to speak what was in my heart.   He didn't put words into my head, he did not cast a spell upon me but allowed the deeper part of my heart to leap forth and once I began speaking what it was I was feeling there was no stopping me. (J)

The Prostitute Story

* * *

I have spoken of this before but it gives me joy because even in Light we can take joy and humor at what has fallen past us.   You refer to my prostitution. Sad to say that was not truth.   I say sadness but because it served much purpose in the teachings of that time and in a round about way for even in distortion of truth can come divine purpose and goodness. Even in the hiding of truth sometimes another truth will make itself known. There was great struggle in early years after his death, struggle amongst those who followed his teachings and those that feared them.

There was division far beyond Judaism and Christianity. Judaism in itself divided many times at that time; other questions, other factors. And with his teachings that he brought from far lands there was even more that developed and grew. Even in those that considered themselves Christians there were divisions of truth and of teachings. Some following the words of one or more of the disciples. Even the disciples bringing their own truth into what they taught. There was a time that women were in an equality of power, where more of the women were stepping up for truth, beginning to learn to read, to write, to teach. There were those who felt it was a problem and were threatened, but more so, were threatened by what was being taught by these women.

The women who followed the teachings of Christ were a bit of rabble rousers in their way and spoke openly against the fathers before them who so long suppressed them. This may have been an error in their thinking and judgement for even in their teachings of Light they held on to the anger and the pain of what was done far before their time. And in doing so they occasionally spoke down on the patriarchal society and the patriarchal teachings which angered many of the men in power, especially the popes.

Mary Magdalene - Miriam

There came a time when people started to move away from the teachings of Christianity and there were many sects of paganism that started to arise again. People were starting to act as though the teachings of the Light were something to fight against. More and more people were rebelling against any power at all and any leaders including the leaders of the Christian faith. Examples had to be set and stories began to arise that began to shift the thinking of the people. One of these stories was that of the prostitute that Jesus forgave. In telling that story the thought was that they could bring the people back around again, those that were sinning, those that were not living the life of spirit. They wanted them to know that they could come back to God, that they would be forgiven for what they had done. In essence was that not a goodly thing? And it did do that so the parable of the prostitute being forgiven, the adulteress, was very powerful and brought people back that felt that they had done the word of God wrong. However, what an opportunity to place women back into the Light of being the source of sin such as the story of Eve. Many steps backward in our growth. So in looking for the name of the adulteress it was asked and who was this woman? Who better than the "apostle to the apostle", to the woman who sat so closely to him, to the woman he revered and that he trusted with his word. Did not that make the story even more powerful, not only was I forgiven but I was sainted - in one lifetime, adulteress and saint - quite a feat even for myself.

Yes, it was a wonderful story and people felt that, "Look how he forgave Miriam." I'm sainted two hundred years before that story arose - I'm de-sainted in one sentence. But good came from it. People understood that the power of God's Light was all forgiving and everything would be forgiven in love. So women and myself sacrificed a bit but only as far as we perceive it to be. If we believe ourselves as less, then are we not? And is it not so that every man has felt that he is less than many times in his life and if he perceives that to be does he not feel that? Change the perception and loose the judgement and allow the Light of God to flow through you. (C)

* * *

Mary Helped Finance the Journeys

Dr. Bezmen asks, "Is it true that you financed some of Jesus' journeys throughout the country?"

* * *

In all modesty and lack of ego, yes, much was financed through the wealth of my family and my inheritance and that man that I was given to in marriage. And I took what was deserved and followed the Christed energy and Light and did indeed finance, as you speak, much of those early beginnings, much of the travel. But I was not the only one who gave and I did not stand at his side because I gave more. There was a bridge of Light that connected us, his words easily flowing as mine, my lack of fear, keeping me steadfast. (G)

* * *

After His Death

Dr. Bezmen asks, "Would you like to share what became of you and Mary of Bethany in the years after

Jesus' death?"

* * *

They were times of much confusion. We all had to carry the teachings. Many of the men had fled. Not all, but many of the immediate followers at first for just cause, of fear for their life and loss of their own families. A few of us remained, at first hiding and then stepping forward. John, who you call the Divine, remained although his heart was broken and his spirit was crushed at the death of his friend. Mary of Bethany was with child and for what many would call lost all shreds of sanity for a period of time. She was taken at one point and we retrieved her again. There was much anger and much fear but much Light that remained. We scattered and regrouped when we could. But his word and his love would not die, it was too much part of us. I eventually grew weary but before my death traveled, I traveled and tried to right some of the wrongs of his trial and of what was done to him by the government. I was still considered a woman of power to some and there was wealth that was still in our reach. I did what I could and eventually gave up life out of despair, out of human weakness, when I grew weary. (B)

* * *

Her Teaching After His Death

* * *

There are many who have received glimpses of that time and they see me often at his side and have called me his wife. I was not his wife. She would have found much fault with that statement but I was a teacher with him. The women were more comfortable speaking with me of their fears and it was I who sat with them and brought the teachings so they could bring it to their children.

The men, some were comfortable with my presence, and some were not. I do not fault them for this and I cast no judgement on them for this for they had learned as their father and grandfathers not to believe and not to trust and not to be open to the words of a woman. Those who opened their hearts completely did not see it as man or woman but saw the words of truth as the words of Light. They were able to see beyond the physical body and to feel the message that was being shared. Yes, I taught with him but my teachings were mostly after his death for many scattered, for many ran, hid and withdrew. Many of the men were the first to run and again I do not fault them. They were seen as a greater threat to those who persecuted us. They were the ones who struggled most with the new teachings, with the new visions.

The women given the gift of speech once again spoke in quiet to their children, took their children to sleep with stories of the Light of God within them and of the man Jesus, Yeshua. I brought the message forward, indeed I spoke to crowds, indeed I went to Tiberias and spoke to him of the injustices surrounding the crucifixion of my friend. Brave, I have been called, I can not claim bravery once my heart flew open and my truth rang out there was no stopping it - it just was! And others, as the shock, as the grief began to lift, as the despair began to turn to hope as he showed himself. As the belief in the promise rang true they were

Mary Magdalene - Miriam

able to step forward once again and many did.   Some
spoke it purely from their hearts, some spoke it from
their humanity and so the stories changed but the truth
remains.   The truth will continue to remain that each
and every one of us is a son and daughter of God, of the
universe. (J)

* * *

Keeper of the Light

*Mary has been called by many titles and she
speaks of two, as does Mary of Bethany.*

* * *

Occasionally I was called Miriam .   Also there
were very many words used.   Some referred to me as the
keeper of the Light.   There was nothing that I kept.   I
just spoke his words, shared all his teachings.   Those he
taught in front of all and those that were meant for a private ear.   He never meant them as secrets. (C)

* * *

*Mary of Bethany speaks of her friend the
Magdalene...*

* * *

Mary does not tell you that she was the apostle to
the apostles after that.   It was she who had the strength
and no one else.   It was she who buoyed up John and
me.   It was she who made sense of everything for us who
showed us the way, who insured that the word continued
to spread.   She was the power behind the throne, so to
speak, in those days and she has never been given credit
for it.   I lived a very long time after that.   I raised the
child that was left for me.   I worked with Mary and with

John in the background and finally died quite old on the island of Patmos. Yeshua, came, he came in the end and took me back with him. (B)

* * *

and the Magdalene adds....

* * *

Yes, I was called by that name. Like many things of our past words are often changed, "apostle to the apostles" was something that was said at a time - actually it was after the time of my death. They referred to me as the one who came and told those who gathered the rest. Did I have any choice? Yes. But when he stood before me and I could feel his presence as clearly as I can feel yours and told me to run and get the others I couldn't find my feet to move any faster upon the earth. Did they all believe me? No. There were those who doubted what I said. There were those who thought that racked by grief that I was without my sense at the time. There were those who resented and felt that I was being chosen, given a gift different than they had. There were those who did not listen to his words, or listened but did not take them within them. All had the ability to see, to feel and to know his presence along with all the other beings of Light who walk this world, who walk the dimensions of time and universe. "Apostle to the apostles"- yes - but more simply, one who followed him - one of many. Maybe I walked a little closer at his side, maybe I had the largest voice. All I know is that his truth rang in my ears and in my heart. (G)

*   *   *

Mary Magdalene - Miriam

CHAPTER FIVE

Jesus the Man

"He was a "god" in man as
we all were and he experienced
every aspect right up to the very
last moment before his death."

Most of the humanness of Jesus has been deleted by current Christian doctrine . Yes, he spent his youth as the son of a carpenter, attended a wedding and showed anger; but his humanity is not central to the purpose we have imposed upon him. History has presented Jesus as the Divine, Only Son of God, to worship. Where they afraid that to speak of his humanity would detract from that image? Did Jesus see himself as that only Son, and was his conception different than other men? - not according to Mary.

Son of God

* * *

Son of God, we have spoken of this before, yes, and all of us were his brothers and sisters, for all of us are sons and daughters of God, sparks of the divine. He wanted so much for those who heard his words to understand that the God he spoke of was the God that resided within them. When he said, "I am the Light", he spoke for each and every one of us. There were those who sat and understood that , "I am" is the God Light of the divine; the spark of each soul and each being that has come into physical form and those that have not. He called upon the angels, the angelic realm and the worker's of Light to be with him. And there are many mentions and yet somewhere through the years, through the ages of mankind, much of this was lost. (G)

* * *

Immaculate Conception

Dr. Bezmen asks, "The church talks about the Immaculate Conception. How do you explain this?"

* * *

All in the writing. To understand what has been written and to understand the teachings is to merely open your heart and your mind. I ask you to look at the world around you now. How many can see the same information, can see the same act and yet interpret it so differently and yet in their heart believe what they see and what they feel to be the truth of what is? So it was during that time, many things were written in many languages. It was not just done in one language. At the time of the death of Yeshua the word of God, the word of the Light was spread throughout many people. He did some traveling, you know, and so did I. Very good times and many different people of many different languages and beliefs listened to what was being said and wrote accounts in their way of what they heard, of what they felt.

Much is lost in translation; much is lost in translation from our language to your language. Is that not truth? Is it easy to see from many languages to other languages some things written in symbols - our language then is very descriptive? Many symbols, many parables were told to teach lessons. This was given to us from our ancestors. Did not our fathers before us speak in parables and stories and words to explain concepts that were so difficult to understand?

Mary gave birth to Yeshua and not in a burst of Light. She labored many hours with joy for she was having a child, a child that she received in a vision. She was guided that this child would be special and one who would hold the Light of God in his heart and be a way shower. Yes, she received a vision, but it was not a dove that impregnated her.

It is interesting that what would be considered pagan by our people at that time is almost accepted in the Christian faith of this time. Yeshua was begotten by flesh with the Light of God within him as it is within you. Was she blessed that she bore this child? Yes. Would you not have and do you not have joy in the accomplishments of your child? She was filled with the pride of a mother, with the fears of a mother for she received vision of what was to come. Not an easy task or thought for any mother who loves their child. A test of faith it was for her, but so pure was her heart that she remained faithful to God in the face of the adversities that would come to her and him. Immaculate was her love for God and her trust in her vision and the angels and the saints that came to her and into those that guided her. (C)

* * *

Jesus Practiced His Faith

We have little choice but to be people of our time. How we are raised, what we are taught and the society we live in forms much of who we are. A few can simultaneously live in their own time and reach beyond to a higher spiritual level. Jesus was one of these.

* * *

You must understand the Hebrew faith, his faith. He practiced, he honored the Sabbath, there was respect for the religion of our fathers and their fathers and many fathers above them. The truths that he followed were not those put down by men but those that were messages from God very much like what you refer to as channeling.

Messages that he received on a mountain as other prophets had also received before him and after him. It was those messages that he followed, that he honored, those that gave honor to God. The laws and the rules made by man as time went on, were those that he disregarded. (B)

* * *

Jesus' Physical Appearance

Had we traveled with him, as did Mary of Bethany and Mary Magdalene, we would have a more complete picture of Jesus. Mary of Bethany, who was his wife and the mother of his three children, experienced his humanity in only the way a lover and wife could know.

* * *

He was a handsome man. He had dark sandy hair. It was lighter than light brown but darker than dark blonde is the only was I can describe it. It was curly and he had very, very deep blue eyes that were rimmed with black. So from even three feet away it looked like he had dark eyes but when you got close they were almost navy, they were very beautiful eyes. He was about, in your measurements, 5-11. He was slender built but muscular. (B)

* * *

Married with Children

A man asks, "I would like to ask Mary of Bethany what happened to the child you had, what was the sex of the child and why we have never read anything about Jesus being married or ever having a child?"

* * *

Those are good questions. There were actually three children. The first child was Rachel and she was about five and a half, almost six when he died. The second child was Daniel, he was almost three. And there was another child on the way when he died and he was named Yisha (ye..sha), which is what I called him. Rachel, after he died, and Daniel were taken by his sister to Egypt for their safety because we were all in a great deal of danger and they studied there for many years. Daniel eventually came back as a young teenager, about thirteen or fourteen years old and joined myself and my brother John and was really raised by John and spent many years with him. Eventually Rachel and Daniel both traveled back across Europe and into England and that is where they died. Yisha stayed in the same area where he was born and after John died took over his position.

You haven't heard about the fact that he was

married for a number of reasons.   Mostly because the writers in the few centuries after his death made him a god, made him more of a god than he was in the sense that we all have god within.   A wife didn't fit; children didn't fit because that would mean he was human.   As the years went on the writers picked and chose what they would tell the world and edited and edited and edited masses of writings. (B)

* * *

Human Stress

Mary of Bethany speaks ....

* * *

It was not planned and yet he knew at some level that when we came back from Egypt that things would never be the same.   He knew it and life changed dramatically after that because he drew people to him like a magnet and he was a man and he became drained many times.   It was difficult, he needed to renew himself, he needed to learn how to be his own person, how to reach out with his heart with empathy and yet not loose himself in it.   He had to learn all the things that we have to learn.   That was a difficult time because I lost him then too.   He belonged to every one then. (B)

* * *

A man asks, "I have been researching the blood-line of Jesus. I am a little confused about the children - I know Mary was with one of them and heard that when they were going to France with Joseph of Ari-

mathea; I was told there was a conspiracy and they were all killed. "

Mary Magdalene also talks of his children ....

* * *

To answer your questions, John, first may I say that it is a delight to hear the questions that evoke the truth of that time.   Indeed, Yeshua had brothers and sisters and indeed he was married and indeed he had children of his own. For those who have never heard these words before let it be known that it is not that your religious leaders have lied rather it has been a sin of omission.   It was not considered important who was to his left and right and who were his lineage.

When his words were being passed to the faith called Christianity, all that was focused on was that which some men deemed were necessary or important.   All the rest was discarded and much of it survives.   The writings of Yeshua, of his wife, of many of his followers, of his children, of his brothers and his sisters do exist and there are many copies that circulate even now.   Bits and pieces, yes, and many times the words have been changed the same way a stone changes as it rolls down a hill losing and gaining, losing and gaining again.

To answer other questions that you had information that all of his children were lost during that time is not correct.   Indeed his children did face transition but not all at the hands of conspirators.   Later on, one child, Daniel, did, but the other children did survive and did move on your planet and in your world to teach and spread the word. Did they announce that they were the children of the Christed one? Highly unlikely! It would not be received well. His son Yisha did teach and did much spreading of the word of the Light. The daughter, Rachel, was very much alive and well but only lived until she was in her young twenties and died after giving birth.

So much information is handed down and comes through many places I can only give you the truth as I know, as I see it, as I experienced and lived it. During that time in France indeed there was much turmoil and indeed there are bloodlines of the man known as Jesus. (I)

* * *

His Personality

Mary gives us an insight into his "less than perfect" humanity.

* * *

Human he was though, and annoyed I did get at him. Sometimes he could be very stubborn, but his love and his belief in what truth was got him out of those entanglements. How do you fault someone who walks in their truth? It was difficult to remain annoyed with him and then there was that smile, that look, that incredible Love, it seemed to have no end like a bottomless well, or the starry fields when you look in them that are endless.

He alone did not possess this and this is what he wished to bring and this in what we continued to bring after his death, those of us who remained. Many of the men ran, I fault them not.   But a few of us remained to go on with the teachings.   Yes, there were followers but the teachers were few.   So it is now.   The challenge of your humanity is for each one of you to be teachers, not followers. Know your truth and know the Light of God. (D)

* * *

Intimacy

In a channeling session Mary was asked if Jesus made love to others and she replied

* * *

Yes.   It is not what can be explained in ways that you will understand.   It was not a group of promiscuous people but a gathering of people who loved and felt deeply and were bound together in ways that are difficult to understand.   Yes, he made love to other people in his life, and yes, he honored his marriage and his love for his wife and yes, I lay in his arms. There were other children, but not by him.   My child was not his. And I would rather keep that in my heart.

* * *

CHAPTER SIX

Those Who Followed Him

"In his day there were other prophets that were also spreading the Light and the word of God: One is known as John the Baptist."

*When we think of the word "disciples" in refer-
ence to Jesus, we often think of the twelve apostles in
the New Testament.   There were many others. In this
section, Mary gives information that makes them more
real and alive to us.   Jesus was a rabbi, a very radical
one who didn't mind speaking his truth even when it
was in opposition to his Jewish faith. To be a follower of
Jesus meant criticism from one's family and neighbors.
From our perspective we see these disciples as fortunate
and blessed to have walked with Jesus but it was not so
in their lifetime. Many of those who spread the teachings after Jesus transitioned were persecuted, tortured
and killed for their steadfastness to those teachings.*

Male Disciples

* * *

All were important and there were many men
that followed at his side.   The men had more difficulty
because of their past training.   To them it was a test of
faith, giving up the life they had known, breaking some
rules of tradition because they could not deny what
was in their hearts or what was in his eyes.   If you
connect with your heart to another's with intent of
Light you will feel his presence stir within you, and it
is so today.   I know you feel his presence, open to his
Light and know your place at his side and at ours. (B)

* * *

*Mary mentions five men who played key roles in
the life of Jesus - - John the Divine, Peter, Judas, John
the Baptist and Joseph of Arimathea.*

John the Divine

* * *

There was one who suffered very much along with us. His John, the one you know as The Divine. His friend, the one he trusted most.   John knew of what was to come for Yeshua.   In his (Jesus') sorrow, his pain, his grief, and in his fear he shared the images of what he was seeing as it was laid out before him to his friend, to my friend, and to Mary of Bethany.

* * *

Mary of Bethany adds a telling fact about John's devotion which was especially important to her as Yeshua's wife.

* * *

Mary of Bethany says.....

* * *

"He, (John), is the only one of the apostles who stayed with him to the very end, all the rest of them disappeared." (B)

* * *

Peter

Though little is written about Peter in the New Testament, his humanity is clearly demonstrated. Since Peter was outspoken, impulsive and fearful, within a matter of hours, he pledged his loyalty to Jesus and then denied him three times. He was driven by his impulsivity to use his sword in the Garden when Jesus was taken by the soldiers. Peter was married since we know that Jesus healed his mother-in-law. Mary tells us that Peter had a difficult time with Jesus' treatment of women as equals.

Peter and Mary Magdalene

* * *

Peter had a difficult time with this.   Poor
Peter, so confused, very often tripping over himself.
He wanted, he longed to hear, "What were the messages, what were the words?"   And in the same
breath, "Why did he speak the words to her?"   As
though I couldn't hear his thoughts.   Peter has come a
long way, ego and pride far behind him. (C)

Peter watched as Yeshua spoke to us in private.
I will not share some of his thoughts of what he
thought was being shared: it was guidelines. (C)

* * *

Judas

The very mention of the name Judas is synony-
mous with betrayer. For nearly two thousand years, it
was Judas, one of the twelve disciples, who has been
blamed for contributing to the crucifixion of Jesus.
Both Mary and Mary of Bethany share with us addi-
tional information, which gives a different slant on this
incident.

Dr. Bezmen asks, "One of the things that you
mentioned when we met for the first time, a while ago,
was that you wanted to share something during the last
few days prior to his death.   It seems that we believe
that Judas had betrayed him.   Is that something that
you would like to address?"

* * *

Yes. Judas took his life for what people had thought, not for what he had done. There were others that betrayed him. There was another that was amidst them that had great fear and was set very much in the old ways that had distaste for the way Yeshua treated women. It was not that he was a bad man. He was driven by fear that what we were following was heresy; what people say now when they follow those of different beliefs as being strange and being against the accepted. Following him was strange and against what was accepted in our day. It was against all the old teachings, as we knew them. There was one who was afraid of where this was leading us all and as the days drew closer to the end of Jesus' humanity, he feared for his life. It was not meant to be a betrayal in the sense that you think of it, it was an act of fear and desperation of the time. Judas did not know why this occurred. He was not the one responsible. He was sent to bring a message, to one he thought to be one of the guards who wore the helmets of the Romans, that believed in us and followed us. He did not betray him although it was said to be like that.

* * *

Dr. Bezmen asks, "How did he get blamed?"

* * *

Because he took the message and he received the 30 pieces of silver. He agreed to take the message in return for the money. Where the one had fear, Judas had greed. He knew there was a lot going on, he knew there was danger but he had no idea what the outcome of this message would be.   He was the one who got caught.   The other one was very, very clever. Judas was a simple man. He bragged about his money and how easy it was to make but then when it all played out and he saw his part he couldn't live with it. (B)

* * *

John the Baptist

* * *

A familiar figure during the time of Jesus in the gospels is John the Baptist. He emerges as a unique character in his attire, his teachings, and his practice of immersion of those that came to him. He stands out as "one crying in the wilderness" and in his connection to Jesus. They were related by blood but even more so in their vision of how to create a relationship with spirit. According to the New Testament, John the Baptist pre-pared the way for Jesus. Mary tells us he did much more.

* * *

It was not until the years went by that the talk-ing of the first John, John the Baptist, as you know him, as your people speak of him, were connected to Jesus.   John anointed, those who came, with water, screaming words of redemption.   Asking those in their faith to question their faith, something was being lost and he knew that.   He was a prophet by his own right in that he could see many things that were unseen by others.   He could see how far we were moving from the truth of faith, from the Light of God, from the one who we call Abba, Father.

He could see that the people were moving in circles, looking for things in flesh, looking for things in wealth, looking for things in redemption that had to do with people, with possessions and losing redemption of themselves. A bit far-fetched, he was at times, but he did get the attention of many. He got mine. I journeyed with friends to the Jordan. I heard him speak many times, not just once. So much made sense and other things I promptly discarded. He spoke of one that was coming. He spoke of one who would understand a truth far greater than he could speak of, one who would be more eloquent than he. Even in his words it seemed so far away, something that was almost like a dream. One man, one human that could speak the words that would make all the pieces of what I had learned fall in place. Could there be such a person? Could there be such a belief that embraced so much of all worlds? (N)

* * *

Jesus Visits the Baptist Many Times

* * *

Jesus said, "Do not wait till death, it will be very disappointing. In so much of your life you can hear the voices, you can know the truth, you can comfort the loneliness and the fear." He admitted that he often had to do that, especially after the death of John the Baptist. And this is the name that you know him of, not always the name that he was called by us. He was a prophet and rabbi and Yeshua went to him, not once, and not for just a few moments, but many times and for many days and weeks to study the new law, to exchange ideas.

That was the seed, the man of the wilderness and Yeshua, the son of a carpenter, talking about things that could not be seen and that could not be touched. And before these days, were not even dreamed to be thought. No one questioned the laws of our people. No one questioned the tablets of stone. No one questioned the tabernacle. All was written and understood. After John was gone there was much work to be done and much more traveling began. (L)

* * *

John and Jesus Together.

* * *

In his day there were other prophets that were also spreading the Light and the word of God. One is known as John the Baptist. Yes, all have heard and have read of him but was he not walking the same path as my Yeshua spreading the Light of God in his way, preparing the way not just for the man but preparing the way for truth? And did he not die as tragically? We often forget about him but I remember the day, standing on the shores and seeing John in the waters. Yeshua was behind us walking through the crowd. He would walk through a crowd undetected except by this enormous feeling of love and comfort. His feet seemed to barely touch the earth. Their eyes are something I have brought with me through time. Anyone who stood on those shores and saw their eyes meet knew in that moment that the Light of God in the universe flowed through both of these men.

They both understood who they were, from where they had come and what their connection was to all that was around them. (D)

Those That Followed Him

* * *

Other Memories of John

Ed Stringham asks, "Can you tell us about the one called the Baptist?"

* * *

I thought you would never ask, John.   No, it is not your imagination nor is it the wild thinking of an active, active thought body.   Nor is it that you ramble in your thoughts as he did but indeed you hold the consciousness of the one known as John the Baptist.

Indeed the memories are there and the connection to all there was and indeed you have embraced Mary of Bethany as friend and held her in your arms in a very special way.   You often asked yourself about the relationship that you have had in this lifetime, how it was different than many that you had seen.   It was not different than the one you had then.   A love that was strong, a bantering of minds and yet you allowed each other to be exactly who you were.   She did not change the man, the man who we delighted in.   The man who said from the human aspect, "This is what God is, take it or leave it, believe it or not, God is, God always will be, God is as strong as the rock I stand on and the staff I hold.   God is as true as what you see with your eyes and that which you don't see."   Yeshua said things in a softer tone and did not pace so.   Pacing and ringing of your hands, Bethany would hold your hands and say, "Hold them still." many times placing your hands on your knee as it bounced as though it was a stallion tripping across the fields.   Many times Bethany called you the wild horse but loved to watch you.   She said to me once, "Look how he tosses his hair like the mane of a pony and yet look at the freedom and hear what he says. Just as the stallion moved across the fields seemingly running into the distance, into nowhere, and yet knowing exactly where he was going." I for one never understood where you were going. In much amazement I sat and wondered were these the rantings of a mad man? I have to admit, Bethany would poke me and say, " listen and look at his eyes. His eyes are the same as Yeshua." Indeed they were.

You both came to deliver the same message. He was not greater than you. That may be difficult for you to understand in your humanity now but Yeshua, the man known as Jesus Christ, was not closer to God than John the Baptist. There were those who could identify with the words of John the Baptist and could understand what he was saying and were drawn to his energy, as you would say. Energy is merely a term that you use for the Light of your soul. I remember the day that we walked to the river and you and Yeshua beheld each other for the first time. I remember you standing in utter stillness. It was the first time, John, that I ever saw you do that, the first time I saw you without words. Tears flowed freely from all of our eyes as we saw your eyes lock, two men in love, in love with the same God, in love with the same message, in love with the same truth. I watched you walk as though the two of you did not put your feet on the earth. I remember having to force myself to see whether or not your feet were on the ground. As you embraced, I swear as I stand in the Light of God, the earth shook.

Those That Followed Him

And you both knew at that moment that your times were limited and that your message had to be spoken but that you would see each other again. And so you did, and so we did, and so we do again.

* * *

Female Disciples of Jesus

The low status of women in the time of Jesus is well known. At the time of the writing of the new Testament, the place and value of women had not changed much. It is assumed, though not known, that the writings in circulation were written by men which would explain why women were seldom included. But the followers did include many women and again Mary Magdalene and Mary of Bethany give us a larger picture of their role as Jesus' followers.

Dr. Bezmen asks, "You told us that there were other women who followed Jesus and I was wondering if you could tell us a little bit more about that? Who they were and how many there were? What were their relationships with him, and for how many years did they follow? Are there people here today with memories of that time?"

* * *

Yes. There are those of you like yourself who walked that path. In his immediate company there were women who stayed at his side for much of the journey. Some as teachers learning in his footsteps, setting out into the crowds and healing. He alone could not heal all the people so the ways were taught to us and we would set forth into the crowds of the sick and lay our hands upon them giving them comfort and love and understanding.　There were many of us that provided what was necessary for travel; preparation of food, the preparation of clothing, the caring of the children that were forever in our presence.　Yes, there were some that were more prominent, but he felt none to be more special than another and no one felt less in his eyes; he had that gift. (B)

* * *

Veronica

Dr. Bezmen asks, "Do you recall any of the names of these women and were you personal friends with any of them?　Did everyone bond together in that group?"

Mary of Bethany answers....

* * *

Yes, we bound together, especially in those of us who traveled with him frequently who never left his side.　There are many writings about Veronica as a mere woman in a crowd who stepped forward; she was one of us.　No stranger to his face or his body, or to his presence.　There was another Mary that traveled with us, and Shushana also. (B)

* * *

A woman asks,　"Roseanne and I both have memories of Veronica and I just wanted to know how we are connected, and a little bit about your and Yeshua's relationship with Veronica?"

* * *

It is good you speak of old friends. It is good for friends to remember and find their truth. Much of what Yeshua taught was the understanding of all that we are. I have spoken and he has spoken of the message of Light, of consciousness that in the mind of God that is so expansive, that holds no boundaries, that has no beginning and no end. As we walk in our humanities, we take on the form of flesh as you see it around you now. As you shed it, as you will, you bring with you so much of what you have seen and touched, tasted, felt, and learned.

And into that Light you go, into many of levels of that Light, for the vibration of God and that consciousness has many houses and you have heard these words. There are many houses, not separate, but on levels of self where all is shared and all is known and before coming back into flesh again or to any other incarnation you choose to bring certain memories and knowings with you. You bring the things you wish to feel, to know, to understand, to share. For what other purpose is there to come into form but to experience a different level of self and to share it in a different way.

Many hold the same memories. It is not uncommon for more than one to glance through the eyes of one who has walked. Indeed you both hold parts of Veronica, and in many ways so different is your humanity but so is it alike, that part of self that remembers. Veronica was in our lives, a young girl at first, and she traveled with us. You have memory of this; both of you hold this in a place in your hearts, not buried in your humanity but the heart that exceeds the body and expands in the places we spoke of.   You saw and you felt, you remember his touch, you remember mine. You remember the laughter and you remember the tears.   You remember his death, you remember that day. The part of you that you have come in this time to resolve, to understand, in humanity, what you could only understand in Light.   The part that was abandoned, the part that was angry and lost. The part that missed his touch.   It is that part that seeks him now.   It is that part that brings you to the greater places within. It is that same part that brings you to the consciousness that you both move into and touch him again, and hold him again, and feel him again.

Remember that nothing is lost and that you were not abandoned.   It is in this lifetime that you remember in your flesh that which you only remembered and knew and understood in spirit in that lifetime.   In this lifetime, you heal those parts of that humanity. Many bring parts of those who walked with him in this lifetime   This is his second coming, bringing him in your hearts, The pieces that walked and laughed and smiled and loved and believed and learned and taught and healed.   And you brought it in many lifetimes and so did I.   Now we remember. Now we step from the pain into the joy   Now we can move from the ecstasy and compassion and love of universal God Light into   the isolation of this flesh and back again.   It is time to bring the memories forward and trust and share.

You two have come together to compare notes because in humanity there is always doubt even when it is screaming before you and within you and around you leaping, from your heart. It is so good to hear the voice of another saying; "I remember that too. We are either both of the same place or crazy." You can choose to believe the latter to come again another time to remember again. This is the lifetime of choice, choose well my friends, my sisters. (L)

* * *

St. Bridget

A woman asks about St Bridget.

* * *

Bridgett indeed, not a tale or a fable but a reality. A woman of God and also a woman of the earth who believed very strongly in the love of the earth and what the earth was giving us who believed in the healing powers of the earth. Not separate from God but saw the earth and all that surrounds as the manifestations of God himself. She took the gentleness of the earth and brought many healings to those that she touched. She was a healer who knew, who connected to, who believed and entrusted in the healing Light that passed through her. Something that you refer to now as healing with touch. She was someone who stood in her truth and stood in the face of fear because of that truth.

She is a strong symbol to those women who connect with earth and with their Light that understand and embrace their humanity and the spirit within them, connecting both halves and both aspects of all that you are.   She will play an important role in teaching you and guiding you if you trust with your heart and ask her for guidance and not depend on what is written of her.   Take her into your heart and see what gifts she has for you. (E)

* * *

CHAPTER   SEVEN

Daily Life With Him and Then, Without Him

"The women cooked and prepared food for those who would come, played with the children, and made ready each journey; gathering the things that would be needed."

The Jesus we know from the New Testament narrative often stands alone even though his followers play their part in the unfolding drama of his life and ministry. Apparently the writers of those gospels wanted to make a distinction between the leader and the group, and eliminating,, to a great extent, the humanity of Jesus as demonstrated in his daily life. It has been said by others, that with the exception of the forty days of temptation in the desert, the rest of what is recorded of Jesus can be reduced to less than a month of time. Much has been left unsaid regarding the daily lives of both Jesus and his followers. We catch a glimpse of the daily routines through Marys' eyes of those days before and after Jesus' death.

New Friends Would Provide

*   *   *

You have many questions as to what our lives were like, what we did. It is not as mysterious as it seems. The women cooked, prepared food for those who would come, played with the children, chastised the children and made ready for each journey, gathering the things that would be needed. There was a knowingness that we had that although we brought provisions and some as myself had a certain degree of wealth we would always be provided for. It was a faith that as we journeyed what was needed would be given to us. There was a divine trust that we had and many of us journeyed with him to lands far before the recorded times and learned the ways of healing and learned all that was available to each one of us.

Yeshua was a gatherer of knowledge, everything he could read, everything he could listen to he did so and made part of himself. He found truth in almost everything that he saw and experienced. He would find that truth and be able to utilize it and express it in words of wisdom and understanding. (D)

* * *

Egypt Story

Traveling to Egypt had an important impact on Jesus and his ministry. The New Testament tells us that Jesus first went there with his parents for safety when Herod decreed that all male Jewish babies under the age of two be killed. Jesus returned to Egypt, at least once, before starting his ministry.

* * *

I must tell you a tale and you can bring it into your heart or discard it upon the earth. There was a time when traveling through Egypt we came upon a house and in that home were those that were not of our faith, that knew nothing of Judaism, of Abraham. And they heard of this man that was walking through with followers and heard tales of healings, of sorcery that was performed and they opened their doors to us not exactly from love or even belief, but in seeking the power and wanting an audience with the great wizard to be known by many to be quite insane. And upon opening that door I first entered as I often did, a little protective I was. And introducing myself to the woman of the house I locked eyes with her. There was a moment of complete stillness between she and I. I knew of her, I had known her in perhaps a lifetime

before or so I thought.   It took a few moments and
there was great silence in the room.   Behind me came
Mary of Bethany with Shushana at her heels.   There
was tension that perhaps this was not the warmest of
welcomes, that perhaps there was danger here.

We sat with one another and she began to speak
of seeing me in her dreams and having visions of a
woman who walked with a man of greatness but he
was in kingly robes with a crown on his head.   And in
her dream he was Egyptian.   His eyes were deep wells
that drew her in and as she shared the dream with me
it became known to both of us that she was seeing the
coming of Yeshua.   She could not imagine a man that
did not look Egyptian for her eyes had never seen one
before.   As he walked through the door she fell to his
feet and he, as always, knelt down to her and lifted her
into his arms.   He spoke to her in a quiet voice that I
strained in my humanity to hear and turned and
smiled his smile to me.   They shared that he had come
to her, that he felt her heart, that he felt her longing to
make sense of all that was happening around her.   He
felt her heart crying out in the darkness and from his
heart he gave her hope.

I share this with you because very often the
Light speaks to us in our dreams and very often the
Light of God comes to us in mysterious ways and in
ways that we will be comfortable, that we will know,
that we can understand.   We must listen with our
hearts and feel with our hearts and open our hearts to
love when love is coming to us.   Needless to say before
long what was once expected in that house was long
forgotten.   There was laughter and there was healing

What Daily Life Was Like

and there was sharing of their lives and of ours. There were drawings upon the earth of the sun and the moon and the rise and fall of the tides and the seas and before long all were brother and sister even from distant lands. See in those that do not look the same as you that Light and that knowing and love and peace and joy will rush through the doors of your heart and sustain you always. (K)

* * *

How They Traveled

Many of us say we believe in miracles or a reality that operates on laws we don't understand. Yet, when we hear a story which violates our known universe, we can be taken back to the land of scepticism.

Dr. Bezmen asks, "Mary, I keep getting visions or feelings that even though you say there was walking I can't believe all of you were walking cross country. Were you using energy to go cross time and places?

* * *

What I might share may at first seem strange but then be drawn into your hearts. It is no mystery that love and Divine Light is an energy of the universe that sustains and supports life itself. There is that which you call altered state where there is no time and when there is very little connection to the physical body to the physical plane. There is movement that is effortless like that in the ancient arts of the orient where simple movement holds the forces of many, where with one breath walls can crumble, wood can shatter. In the energy of that Divine Light and in that state of Love, and in that unity of one another, movement was effortless.

To the eye we walked to many places with feet barely touching the earth.   There was no condition of physical body that prohibited long distance.   Days seemed like moments, weeks seemed like a blink of time.   It is hard to understand what you can not see. You can transcend different levels.   There are degrees of movement and of reality.   That which appears to you and then disappears crosses thresholds.   We could move in the same way.   This is possible, this is known. If you open the deepest part of your heart and mind and expand out your awareness you can travel to the infinite.   Some of our movement was not in third dimensional body and some was. (K)

*   *   *

Walking with Him

*   *   *

I gazed through those same eyes.   I remember once I shared this story with you, dear friend.   I remembered once I found him, I met him and my life was a whirlwind of what I was taught to believe, of what I doubted, of what I feared, and of what I was now hearing and learning from him.   Opposite ends of the universe - all that I could not receive into my heart was now flowing in.   I came from a life of pain and anger, of feeling abandoned by God, by my father, by my family.   I questioned the existence of God who abandoned me and allowed me to suffer and to be confused, to be criticized and judged by so many and now here was this man turning my life inside out and upside down. It was wonderful, it was frightening, I tried to run from it, I tried to deny it, I even begged that it be taken from me and I began to see angels of Light, seeing things that were not there, as though I ate those berries that we were warned against that brought you to wild and mysterious places and you woke up with a pain in your head and an ache in your abdomen. A drug, an intoxication that came from his words.

I often looked at the food that we were preparing to make sure that nothing was slipped into it, not that I doubted. And I would gaze at a reflection of myself in water, in ponds and rivers, and did not recognize who I saw. I could not see anymore a person that I found unattractive. I could not see the part of myself that I judged and it got so that all I could see were my eyes - a Light dancing in them. And in those eyes I could not see the sadness. All I can say to you is embrace it, (your Light), because once the doors have opened do you want to walk back? Do you want to go back? Scary and wonderful and so full of feeling. Why in our humanity do we avoid the feel of all of it? We avoid the pain, we avoid the sorrow, we avoid the joy. The truth is all of it gives us our aliveness, gives us our passion.

I ask you, all of you, the greatest passion you have ever felt sometimes has lied in words or poems or stories or songs that has sadness and grief and pain. Has it not stirred you to feel? And in that place we open our hearts to seek the greater love and to seek comfort if we can learn to feel the sorrow. If we can learn to be in fear and seek out the comfort of Light and of Love we have reached enLightenment. Each time we push past the pain and surround ourselves in unshakable passion and comfort, Light is with us. Continue to walk and we will walk with you. (K)

I have been asked by many to speak of those times and many come to hear to what it was to walk with him, with us.   What it was like for a group of people to walk in their truth, to speak from their heart, and I will speak of this but is it any different than what it feels like when you step into your truth, when you speak from your heart that is so full.   The tears well in your eyes because the words don't come that you can't find them to express what you are feeling, that is what it was like to walk with him.   That is what it is like to know the wholeness and the completeness of self, to finally stop the senseless, endless pain and suffering we bring upon ourselves and embrace the idea that it does not have to be - that God does not cause or create the suffering.

Although in humanity, and even in ours, we curse God for that suffering and one another.   We had at least the faith, the safety of slipping back in that place, into that safe harbor of His love and the memories of him as man struggling with humanity and always seeing the God Light.   And if he could do it so could we; or so that was the message.   Where is that message now?   Where has it gone?   Can you find it in your heart to hear it, does it have ears and eyes and a voice to speak for it is truth?

We walked with him and we watched him die, the craziest of all times, the insanity, we felt it coming,

we saw glimpses of what might be, we heard the rumblings of the crowd, we heard the voices in the night,
the messages were passed. You could smell and taste
the fear even in our sleep. The doubt of humanity rising and falling and then the touch of his hand. It did
melt me. I could get so frustrated with him, wanting
him to save himself, to stay in the humanity that we
held so dear. Even through his words and messages it
is in our humanity that we cling to that which we can
touch and feel and hold. It is not a fault, it just is, and I
did not want to let him go, none of us did. And each
one of us felt it so differently and yet the same. The
men angered and cursed at themselves, the elders, the
Romans, looking for a place to blame and even Him.
Why was he walking this path? Why was he choosing
to speak instead of silence and silence instead of speaking? It is said in your humanity ripples of words that
have been written by those who are very wise, "That
which does not destroy us makes us stronger." This is
one way to understand those days for some were
destroyed, shaken, frightened, nowhere was safe.

Once Yeshua drew his last breath there was
safety nowhere. The safety of his touch was gone, the
comfort of his eyes could not be seen, his flesh could not
be felt as we anointed and wrapped him that last time.
And yet some place so deep we knew that it was not
over. I say again and I have said before because it is
so important that this message be heard: His body did
not disappear, it did not evaporate into the sky. We
removed it, we took it to safety and you must understand why that had to be done. There was a belief
that stayed in all the faiths, not just among the
pagans, that in every cell of the human body there

existed the essence of the soul of that person.   He
would have been desecrated, he would have been torn
and divided, his flesh would have been sold, his bones
would have been broken, for this was the way of the
time.   This was the fate of all those prophets and holy
ones to walk before him and we could not allow this to
happen, this could not be, not with him.

There were too many who did not understand
his words even amongst his followers.   There were
those who were seeking power and fame because they
had been seen by him and in his company. Not all was
Light and yet not all was Darkness and yes, he did
appear and yes, it was to me - so the stories are correct.
Some of the men who held the pen managed to put
words of truth on paper as showing himself in spirit
was a comfort to all of us. A knowing that he did not
disintegrate. His body, the consciousness, the truth,
the Word continues as we would, that there indeed was
a soul without beginning and end; a journey in the universe of Light, of eternity where all would be known to
us and understood.   And to many of us it gave great
faith and hope and courage because the loss we knew,
that on drawing our last breath, it was not the last and
it was not for nothing - that love, that passion can be
felt.

I could feel him, we could all feel his Love pouring like rain on dry ground we drank it into our hearts
and into our flesh. It filled us, it quenched the thirst, it
filled the hunger.   We still missed his touch but I did
not loose him nor did any of us and he showed us not
only himself but others that we loved and that loved us
- that he was not God but a part of God's Light and so

What Daily Life Was Like

were they and so were we.   I even saw those in Light that I did not expect to see.

Forgiveness, yes! Judgement did not exist - it only laid in the hearts of our humanity and had no place in Light. This was another lesson which you call a teaching that we could rejoice for there is no judgement in the eyes of God. You are living your humanity and when you live it from your heart and your truth that is all that you are expected to do - that is your purpose - that is your life.   In the days, the weeks, the months that passed many hid and I admit in my humanity I judged them knowing that at some time I would find the peace of forgiveness and I set out with John, with Mary and we went many places. We left the city and moved just in the stillness of night, we moved into places where we could continue to speak the truth.   We traveled to distant lands and spoke of Him and many listened.

His children grew, Daniel, the oldest of his two sons came into this world with memories of other places. He remembered the stars in the universe and gazed into the night understanding the infinite. Rachel, her heart danced with Light and joy. She had her mother's childish ways but really more Light hearted. She could break into a smile that would melt hearts and heal. She spoke to her father often. The dear child could not know the difference that he no longer had a body. She saw him so clearly and felt him so strongly that she never mourned. Yisha carried strength and his father's fight and stubbornness.

So much occurred in those days, so much was

learned and shared, so much was accepted, so much was cast away.   Throughout the ages time has changed so much of the words that were meant to be heard in the hearts of all.   In the stillness you can hear those words.

Mary now addresses the audience

I come to speak to all humanity. My message this evening is about women. It must be understood, know your rightful place, understand the beauty and the God Light that lies within you, understand the equality of all.   So many times, so many places, the suppression of women has occurred only to rise up to the suppression or the disdain of men. Do not fall into this trap. You do not have to put down one to honor another. You do not have to step upon those who have stood on the joy of the female energy. It is what was learned, it was fear.   It was taught and promoted throughout the ages from the beginning of Eve through my time and far beyond. It was the fear of women that caused all of the grief, all the suppression and all of the pain.   We are neither superior nor inferior, we are brother and sister.   We are children of God - we are equal and passionate and compassionate and we can teach one another so much of that place in our hearts.

Allow yourselves to remember, to remember the love, to remember the joy, to remember the touch, the touch that did not rise you above others but have you stand side by side, hand in hand, heart to heart in one luminous Light.   There are many questions; I will answer all that you ask. Do not fear to ask. (K)

*   *   *

What Daily Life Was Like

CHAPTER   EIGHT

Preministry

"It was in Egypt that it was clear
that he had come willingly from the
father (God), to change the
thinking of many and to bring
them back themselves. To bring
the freedom that they were looking for into their hearts."

Those familiar with the New Testament know that there is approximately an 18 year gap between the time when Jesus was twelve, in the temple, and when he started his ministry at the age of thirty. There has been much speculation, but we may assume that Jesus was having spiritual experiences that would prepare him for the last three years of his life; his ministry. Mary Magdalene and Mary of Bethany give some insight into this period of Jesus' life.

Jesus as a Young Man

* * *

Yes, I can speak of that time. Was I with him? No. But being transcended of Light, all is known to us now. He was a precocious child, questioning all, listening to all. He sat with the teachers, the rabbis, he listened. He also listened to the words of his father, Joseph, his wisdoms. As he grew, he began to question more and more what was being taught for many of the words spoken did not feel right to him. As a child he had very many visions. He was warned by his mother and father to speak softly of the visions he had received and only to certain ears. They did not discourage his questioning nor did they discourage his visions but taught him the art of when to speak and when to listen.

He began to travel with his uncle and also with his father. At first, not to distant lands but learning of his people, learning of his faith, of his heritage and of the teachings that fell before him. You could always see in his eyes the questioning, constant thought, constant thought. And as he grew older by the time he was a young man and coming into age, the age of the blessings of manhood, he had complete knowledge of his faith, more interests than other young boys were expected to learn. More questions than he could ask. A vision was given to his uncle, his mother and his father that he was to travel and to learn of the faiths of others, to learn the teachings of the Light of God through the writings of other people. It became clear to him, even in his own faith, that words from one man to another did not always match. His hunger to compare, to learn, to know grew stronger and stronger and so they traveled, journeying many years, returning home and journeying again. It was not done in one trip, as some would have believed. Interesting, so close to the truth and yet so far. They traveled to different parts of the world farther than those that could conceive could be done. It was customary to travel beyond your own land, beyond the land of your ancestors at least, not of Hebrew faith. He traveled into Egypt; he traveled into the Far East. The continent and the people do not lie the way they do now. It was not as far as one may think now.

The seat of humanity rose heavily in the area of Egypt and spread out from that point. Distant lands were not as distant as you may think but yet farther than anyone had traveled in his time of his people. He learned of other practices. He learned of mysticism. He learned that other people had visions such as he, such amazement of finding someone in another land, in another language with visions such as he had. He learned much and came back to his people collecting followers along the way, bringing teaching, bringing knowledge and adding to what was known. He wanted others to question as he did.   Some did, some did not, especially when he was a young man. (C)

*   *   *

His Travels and Other Religions

Jesus traveled to foreign lands. He studied man religions and held each in reverence.

*   *   *

Oh, he had great respect for them (other religions).   He felt that we had gone so far away from them, from the power of the earth and universe, from the source of all healing. All of these so called primitive religions all had the same core; to draw healing energy from your source of all healing and share it - as simple as that.   That is what he brought back to us, that is what he taught us and that is why he taught the children how to heal, because they had not guile, they had not been corrupted, so to speak. You have no idea how many hundreds of children learned how to heal during his lifetime. His own children were teachers of the other children, little Rachel especially. She was a master healer even though she was only a little child.

Yesh traveled far and at great cost and at great exhaustion at times to learn the ways of many, to see the Light and all the truth and to honor anything that gave honor to source. He honored the earth beneath his feet, the sky, the water. Healing was of mind and body and of spirit. He taught us to open our spirit in any way that we felt we were connected to. We drew in God's Light, the ritual mattered not. (B)

*   *   *

Preministry

Where They Studied in Egypt

* * *

There were many schools. Some were looked down upon by the people in power. There were schools of mysticism as it was referred to. Some of these schools we attended. Most had names that would serve no purpose. They were held in courtyards, they were held in fields. The secreted ways of the learned were passed from one to another. For most of those ways, in schools, women were not a part of until he came. We learned in those places how to feel the Light within us and how to remember our connection to all that there is. How to move what you refer to as your energy, your essence of life, what makes you breathe as you are in this physical form and will continue after physical form is gone. (B)

* * *

Mary of Bethany adds more information about these travels.

* * *

Between the ages of approximately twelve to twenty six he traveled across what is now Europe into what is now Great Britain, England and to Ireland and he studied there. He studied all those what were considered primitive religions. And then he also went the other direction to India, he studied Hinduism, he studied Buddhism. There was not a major philosophy in the world that he was not aware of and did not know intimately. And he was only home for about a year at the time I met him and then his last period of study was almost three years in Egypt. And from Egypt he came back and began his public life.(B)

* * *

Jesus' Soul Purpose

*   *   *

It was there he learned his soul's purpose.   It was in Egypt that it was clear that he had come willingly from the father to change the thinking of many and to bring them back themselves.   To bring the freedom that they looked for into their hearts.   It was a joyous time in Egypt and a painful one for from that moment it was on his face and in his eyes of things that were to come. (B)

*   *   *

Mary of Bethany adds...

*   *   *

He knew.   He knew at a very deep level but he didn't know the details, he truly didn't.   He came here to be man and all that that means.   It meant fear, it meant anger, not exactly when or how or what would happen.   In a way his knowing was like a cloud over his head because he knew it would be painful and unpleasant and yet he knew it would also be his final knowing of what it was like to be man. It also meant happiness.   All the human emotion and that not knowing his future in the sense of anticipation.

*   *   *

The Magdalene continues...

*   *   *

It seems as if he came here to experience everything that man could the same way he studied each of the religions, each of the belief systems that were on the planet that he was to live life fully. (B)

*   *   *

The Beginning of His Ministry

Jesus the student was preparing to become the teacher.

* * *

It happened very slowly, it was not what he planned. It brings joy to my heart to remember those days. I remember he became more serious but still had joy in his heart when he found his soul's purpose. I remember asking him, "How does it feel to know? You seem to know just what to do and where to go and where it's carrying you." And he answered, "I have not all the answers but what is your soul's purpose Magdalene? What brings your soul into my presence, what brought your soul to this life?" It was something I worked on for many days and weeks afterwards.

He wanted us all to know to search out why we were here and what it was we were to learn and do. He encouraged us to see the God Light within us, as we were all brothers and sisters coming from the same Father as he. When we started to journey backward to the land of our fathers, our earthly fathers, the people came, the numbers gathered. Somehow as we reached a town or a village, they knew we were going to arrive and were waiting; many with curiosity, many with fear, many with anger, many that were ill and hoping to be healed and looking for what were called miracles, but were merely healings of the heart and of the spirit. The numbers grew. He did not enjoy the things that people called him or the burden of so many so quickly and yet he opened his arms and his heart and turned away no one.

* * *

Jesus as Role Model

* * *

He had wisdoms deep within his heart and an ability to understand, to always know when to speak and when to listen. He also knew when to speak and when to listen to his Father. He had a Light within him and as he traveled people followed that Light because they felt it was in themselves. They followed him not so much for who he was but for what he made them feel in themselves. Yes we went to Egypt, we went to many places and we learned the ways of healing, healing of the soul, healing of the body, it was a very long journey and many things happened along the way. Many people healed in the Light of God. (B)

* * *

Those that Traveled with Him

* * *

We all traveled with him; there were many that came, the numbers changed, from town to town, people would follow and listen. It was not meant to be public appearances, rather a sitting of minds and an exchange of thoughts, a giving of love. He enjoyed sitting with people and learning from them and as we traveled he was open to all that he saw and all that he heard. He drank it in like a sponge would take on water. He would take on people, their beliefs, their joys and their sorrows. (B)

* * *

Jesus as Rabbi

Jesus was a rabbi, but was he the only Son of God as most Christian religions proclaim? Mary Magdalene and Mary of Bethany provide their views.

A man asks, "I have a lot of questions. I am just starting to learn about Jesus' life. I was brought up Jewish and it is really confusing for me. If Jesus was teaching Judaism why we don't learn about him and you? It's not even mentioned.

Mary Magdalene answers.....

*   *   *

Not a simple question and yet the answers are very simple. All that know the name of Yeshua know him to be rabbi, know him to be one of the faithful Jews of Israel, one of the faithful teachers and followers of God. This is spoken of in the writings of Judaism as well as in the writings of Christianity and many other writings. What happens to truth and to the words as they pass from humanity to humanity? In humanity each soul has the ability, the right of interpreting their own truth. Ego, power, seeking truth in things other than the Light has brought very many men to crimes, to acts of unthinkable horror. Although the hiding and destroying of information, of writings, is not considered a crime by most, it did stop the information from passing from mind to mind. However, the Light that has its place in all men has access to that information.

Yes, he was rabbi, and yes, I was of good faith

and so were his followers, not unlike sects of Judaism that exist today, and do they not argue amongst themselves as to how to practice the law of God, even now? They have not stopped condemning even amongst themselves. Christianity did not stop the fighting, the ego and the distortion of truth. That it set to change those who established a difference from Judaism created their own havoc, their own egos, their own crimes of hiding truth. Look at what is referred to as the Crusades. Were there any greater crimes spoken in the name of God, of Light, created by men seeking power? In their truth, they sought the power of God and faith; in that truth they were walking the path of God. I do not condemn them but it is a lesson for humanity.

There were those who would benefit by losing information. Has that changed even in this world that you live? Is not information lost and found, distorted to create a reality of the hands that hold it? Can not every man have the capacity to create truth through manipulation, through ego?

Things have not changed. Things have also not changed that there is just as much Light as ever, just as much truth as ever. And many, many more find their vision within and look through the eyes of that vision to what is being presented to them and ask, "Is this my truth?." It did not serve the purpose of a patriarchal society to have my writings hanging about. Of Thomas, so despondent they were, because they knew that his writings contained information about the quality of man and woman, their quality of Light, the abolishment of barriers of class between people. We watched the writings be preserved after we went into Light with the others and rejoiced as they were placed in safe keeping and were saddened when the eyes that fell upon the writings did what they may with them. Even in these jars most of these writings have been put aside. It is fascinating and human nature. The part that we experience, that although the writings were not wanted they were not destroyed. What stopped the hands of these men from destroying the writings that they feared? Why did they wrap them, maintain them and hide them away? Was the Light within them still guiding them even though their minds chose differently? Was there a greater force, a Light that drove them to maintain and preserve that which they feared? As you grow in Light and as the information is revealed the answers you seek will be answered. (C)

* * *

Mary of Bethany speaks...

* * *

We understood that this was a very holy man, a master teacher who would save us, who would lead us out of bondage in the sense that the Jews for many centuries had had a very difficult time. And many people felt that he would be like a king and that the tables would be turned, that the Romans would no longer be in charge and somehow the Jews would take over and be respected for what they were.

The Essenes were a group of Jews who had prepared for centuries for his coming. That had been prophesied. And there were many women, my mother, my aunt, his mother, his grandmother who had been preparing and waiting and watching. And so when he was born there was a small group who knew, or at least felt that he was the one that would lead them and become their king and so when he came back from traveling people would draw around him just as they did in years to follow.

* * *

Dr. Bezmen asks, "Did Yesh at any time believe he was the Son of God?"

* * *

Not in the way it has been interpreted. He knew his soul's purpose was that of a higher calling as many masters and those of the Light have come to this planet before to this earth. He knew his task was to bring his Father's Light to all and to recognize that each one of us has that same Light and connection. He reminded us from where we came and from whom we were part of and taught us to honor all the living things around us that were also full of God's Light. Yes, indeed he was the son of God as I am his daughter! (B)

* * *

CHAPTER NINE

The Teachings of Jesus

"Simple truth: We are all brothers and sisters in God, we are all children of the Universe, all sparks of that Divine Consciousness."

When we listen to the Magdalene we learn about the teachings of Jesus through the heart, mind and soul of another. What we hear brings us as close to Jesus as we have ever been, for Mary was his confidant and a powerful force in the early Christian movement. Some of what she reveals parallels traditional beliefs, yet the core truth of those messages is often different. Mary shares information that is either unfamiliar to us and sometimes she presents ideas that are in opposition to traditional beliefs. In the beginning of this section, there are a few brief passages which summarize the heart of Jesus' teachings.

"Simple Truths"

* * *

There were some simple truths. The Light of God resides within every soul. Simple truth, we are all brothers and sisters of God, we are all children of the universe, all sparks of that Divine consciousness. Truth that the greatest challenge of your humanity is to bring that Light into your humanity and live it to its fullest; to raise the vibration of this planet by raising the vibration of each person beginning with self. Truth; God holds no judgement, the universe holds no judgement; that judgement is an act of your own humanity and it is enough that each one of you do it to yourself - that is your darkness. Your Light is when you bring compassion to that judgement and elevate it to Light. Mary of Bethany was his wife, I was his dear friend, as many, I the largest "mouth" of female energy that walked with him. (G)

* * *

Other Teachers of Light and Love

* * *

You just need to acquire the knowledge of the existence of Light, of something so far greater than what you see and what you feel. Yeshua is not the only one that speaks this truth. Countless millions recognize the Love of God, of the universe, of the One, by any image they hold in their heart. Some spoke of it in quiet ways, names you will never read on pieces of papyri, names you will never see written in stone. There have been countless thousands of sparks of Light who recognize the Light of the One. (C)

* * *

Why He Came

* * *

It is good to once again be able to share some of the truths of our time. It is in the sharing that we hope that the minds and the hearts of all the souls of the earth can begin to open to their own truth. It is for this purpose that he came, and many like him, for he who is known as the Christed one was not the only one to walk this earth, to spread the Light of God and the Light of truth. But in his lifetime, and because of the events that occurred around it, it is he who is looked to as the example of that Bringer of Light. He gets great joy and pleasure at those who see the Light of God in others eyes and recognize it not to be in one man.

This is happening more now in your universe, in your world, in your time. When the Light within you shines so freely that it is open and sees in others the same divinity. It is truly a joyous time for all of us who walked with him, as many of you here did. For those that are gathered for these messages often walked at his sides. In one way or another they are drawn to the words, are drawn to the memories in their hearts and in their minds, questioning, "Is it what I think, is it possible that the words that have been written may be wrong? Do I perhaps own part of the truth?" This is so. We speak often about what is occurring in humanity. There are many guides and guardians who come to this planet now to try to give some comfort, wisdom, understanding. I come and I speak to bring the understanding by explaining what once was and how in essence it is no different now. Yes, it is so. (D)

*   *   *

How He Taught

*   *   *

Many hours were spent in that lifetime that you were present, sitting and writing many of his teachings. We would sit by the lamps in the quiet and still of the night, gather around him, and he would ask us many questions. One of the things that he had asked of us was to write down those things that connected us to one another. What were those actions that made you feel validated in your heart, your connection to another? Was it when you looked into their eyes? Could you look into the eyes of another and send forth your heart love? He looked for those things that were not great. He would often have us write and we would try to come up with the grandest things that we could do for another. "Oh Rabbi," we would say, We can take in the orphans, we can work in the field until there is not Light to feed the starving." Each one of us would try to come up with the grandest things that we thought that God would want from us. And not that these things do not have value, but he would say very gently, "Have you smiled at your child today? Have you touched your lover? Have you put your arms around an elder and let them feel humanity and the comfort of being held? Have you sent a loving thought to one who is very difficult to love? I ask you when you think you do not do enough, when you think there is more that you are to do to list all the quiet moments when you send the Divine Light, the Light of God to another. The paper you have chosen is not long enough. Even by sending love to living things around you, you do the work of God. When you embrace your own frailness and do not judge yourself, your own weak humanity, self, you have done a deed of good. Every act of kindness to self is an act of God."

Do you know why rose quartz was brought to you? It is to open your heart to receive, to find within you the worthiness to receive the love of God that pours to you always . Open your heart to embrace and to know that you are not judged. (J)

* * *

Teaching Together

Mary tells how she and Jesus taught together as Jesus, in spirit, is close at hand.

* * *

First, he speaks of me and thanks me for acknowledging him. This is something that he has done in the past. Many times I would be teaching. I would be speaking his words and he would come gently behind me placing his chin on the top of my head acknowledging the words that I spoke and I would do the same to him. And he does that to me now. He tells me that there are some of you that feel his presence now that have no doubt that his love is with you. He holds in his hand a symbol that he had shown us during that time. He had drawn it in the sand and then raised it up and holding the sand in his hand he opened his hand and there was a beautiful crystal a stone with many facets. He spoke to us of the Light of God being present before he brought this word. He showed us of times before Abraham and before Moses that the Light of God and his Light shown brightly in this universe. This crystal takes form and shape and that has been spoken of before. There are a few that exist on earth at this time. Many look to a form referred as the "skulls" for answers and truth and indeed they hold some of what people are looking for, what humanity seeks, connection to the universe and connection to the all.

But he shows me now a smaller stone that within it has a ray of blue Light. This stone carries a Christed energy that was present during the time of what you refer to as Atlantis and has shown itself again on your planet. In the blue color in the center of this stone is the ability to heal many things. When I speak of healing, and as he speaks, it is not of the flesh but the spirit. For those who hold this crystal, this stone, the struggle is over. Those who hold this stone know at once the Light of God that is within them. He has not shown this to me in a long time and my memory has almost forgotten it. He plays with it showing me with a joy and with laughter how simple things can be. The message that he brings in addition to the symbol is that many have been called together now in his name and not in his name as a man, and not in his name as a God , but as the energy of the universe, the Christed Light, that Light which holds the love, the compassion, the power to heal, the power to connect, the power to unite all beings. It is being summoned forward now. Many who walk with him are being called together now. He stands beside me with his hands open wide calling all in this room before him to remember and to fear not. He will be with you as sure as the sun shines on the earth and warms your skin. His love pours to you now, embrace it and remember.(I)

* * *

The Spiritual Equality of Women

With few exceptions it was believed that God talked primarily to men. Women and children were ignored. Jesus diverted from traditional religious beliefs as he included women and children when he taught. This was often met with opposition and derision.

* * *

There were many schools. Some were looked down upon by the people in power. There were schools of mysticism as it was referred to. Some of these schools we attended. Most had names that would serve no purpose. They were held in courtyards, they were held in fields. The secret ways of the learned were passed from one to another.

Women were not a part of those schools, of the inner learning, until he came. Though we did learn in those places how to feel the Light within us and how to remember our connection to all that there is.   We learned how to move what you refer to as your energy, your essence of life, what makes you breathe as you are in this physical form and how you will continue after physical form is gone. We would expand upon that and feel our connection with God as Yeshua felt his.

It was in Egypt he learned his soul's purpose. It was there that it became clear that he had come willingly from the father to change the thinking of many and to bring them back themselves, to bring the freedom that they looked for into their hearts. It was a joyous time in Egypt and a painful one for from that moment it was on his face and in his eyes of things that were to come. (B)

*   *   *

The Equality of Light

*   *   *

Yeshua and I had many conversations about bringing the two concepts together, about having each man and each woman see only the Light that was the same within each other, recognizing the strength, learning from the strengths of one another, to make that Light grow brighter and brighter. (C)

*   *   *

Women Embraced His Words

*   *   *

I followed him and so did many others. There were more than twelve. Many followed. We prepared meals together, we sang, we danced, we shared our stories, our thoughts of life, of the universe and of the stars above us. And he would sit and within one or two words bring a clarity to those questions. It wasn't how many words he spoke; it was what we felt in each word that was spoken. All made sense. We learned to hear with our hearts, not our heads or our ears but listening with senses that rose so deeply and knew the truth. (D)

*   *   *

Self Empowerment

Dr. Bezmen looks for clarification. "It sounds like he taught self-empowerment?"

*   *   *

Very much so - he taught remembering, he taught going inside and getting in touch with the God within. He taught that we were no different than he. Perhaps he had an awareness that was more expanded in some ways but that we were no different; that we were as much God as he was. That was what got him into trouble later. (B)

*   *   *

How He Taught Children

*   *   *

I will pass to you what I observed in him. Indeed he had a way with children. My heart grows so large at the image of him with the children. He was present with them. He would sit with very few words. I always waited for more words; I would anxiously wait to hear what he was going to say to the children, what message he was going to bring, what parable, what story was behind his eyes. And instead, I would first be met with the presence of love with that gentle look as he would look into their eyes.   The corners of his mouth would soften and he had a smile that is difficult to create and now that I think of it was the smile of a child, effortless, without thought.   It moved across his face and danced.   He watched them and as they were running circles around him, trying to get his attention, and often behaved in manners that were not quite acceptable.   He would watch and with a look on his face the child would stop and be caught in his expression and then with very gentle words he would begin to bring that child closer to him the way the fishermen would throw out their nets.   First he set out a net of love.   He cast it out and then without their being aware he gently reeled them in.   They did not fight against the net for it did not hold them tight.   The net became a place of safety as they drew closer - they did not fear the words that were going to come forward.

I expected him to say what they were doing was not acceptable but the first words that came from his lips were how beautiful they were, how their eyes danced like stars, how they moved about as quickly as ants gathering crumbs that had fallen to the ground. They would begin to laugh and then very gently he would begin to speak to them of what was good and what was truth.   If they were misbehaving he would speak of the opposite, of the peace and the joy of how it felt to be loving.   He would tell them stories that embraced the goodness that was within them.   He would feed that until it was greater than any deed that they had done.   He had the Light rise in them until it overpowered the shadow on the ground.   He did not, in any way, support the behaviors that were not acceptable but in his words it was clear and when he had to say something - when there had to be a ceasing, if a child was hurting another, the words just came from his heart. They spoke not from the lower of his body and not from his mind but from his heart. Words spoken from the heart are heard louder than any other words. So if you must correct, if you must teach, take the words from your mind and breathe them into your heart. Let your heart surround them in Light and love and then let them fall from your mouth. They will hear the lesson and they will feel the love. (J)

* * *

His Teachings and Acceptance

* * *

Lost and found many times only to be enjoyed, to discover those facets, those parts of you that hold so much in truth, in life. That which you seek without the desperations of the eternities, of humanity, striving so hard lying within you, tiny little memories and sacred places within your heart. Yeshua came to open the doors to those sacred places. This is what he spoke of, "Arise and awaken my brothers and sisters," he would say. "Arise from the sleep, come from the land of forgetting and know who you are, the Divine Lights of the eternal God."

It didn't always go over very well. That wasn't the belief. There were those that doubted and those that feared and those that went along knowing that there was truth in the "insanity" of the thoughts. How insane was it for any man or woman of God that walked at that time to believe that we had God within us? How insane it was, how blasphemous it was, to think that we were equal to that which we revered, to that which we held so separate from ourselves? Indeed it was the rebels (who embraced his teaching); those that dared to ask themselves, those that dared to believe their dreams and allow their dreams to manifest into the reality of their life.

And so his followers came, as I did, as you did, as all in this room did. Many who are walking this earth now walked in the consciousness of that time. We cannot all be connected and yet be separate from our thoughts, so indeed, as you return to Light do you not share the memories of all? Do you not see and know through the eyes of God, do you not bring that with you? It may not have been the eyes that you look through now that saw Yeshua, that saw the Light in his eyes and felt the Love in his heart, that walked the earth with the feet that you walk now. But the part of you that is much greater than what you see, what you beheld, did walk, did see, did hear the words of truth and they rang in your heart. For all the steps you have taken in this lifetime have led you to these words now. Have you not asked yourself why have you been brought before these teachings, these concepts, these ideas? Are there not many others on your planet now, in your humanity that never behold or hear what you do at this moment? Yes, you return, and return again, and again. Not even I was allowed to stay in the land of the sleeping, nor would I choose to.

Spirit, Light, eternal Love and compassion is what we bring not only to this planet but to this universe. It takes shape and forms in many ways. As many guides have spoken of in your humanity you will still see yourself as just here and now, elitist, the concept of other consciousness connected to the Light of God connected throughout this universe. In your intellect you may have accepted but does it dwell in your heart? And how many other places have you experienced others in this planet, other than your world as you see it? Yeshua gazed upon the stars and had us look up and asked us to see all that we are and know all that we have experienced and in a moments time we were traveling through those stars like birds of flight. Sorcerer some said, work of the devil, a magician that he makes us leave our bodies, that he makes us have illusions.

Many walked away from truth; many stayed, as we did, embracing every word as we felt it in our hearts, knowing the sound of truth as it was spoken. Indeed we were all brothers and sisters and we saw through his eyes the Light of each one. So easy it was to shed the humanity, to forgive, to understand it and to embrace it more. We would gather at night and speak of what we thought and what we did in our humanness and we did so from the place of spirit like playful children.

Instead of condemning our humanity and judging each other we looked at our humanity as we would look at children at play, amazed at what we said, at what we thought, at what we did. And understanding it was the innocence of not knowing the greatness of the Love of God. We took ourselves so much lighter. Not only did we embrace ourselves as children and delight even in our failings, even in our antics, even what was perceived to be the wrong decisions, but we were able to embrace the children even more. And the children did flock to him. No, it is not just in the hands of artists that drew pictures through time but indeed children found comfort in his arms and in his love and in all of us.   For as we embraced ourselves how effortless to embrace the children.   How easy to help them remember, from the beginning, who they were.   Are you not challenged every moment of every day to seek who you are? Allow your minds to remember, yesterday, last week, a year ago and then further through the sands of time, through the dimensions of time and bring yourself back to the Light of God. There you will find the comfort you seek and those that have passed before you with open arms. (H)

*   *   *

Crystals as Time Capsules

Mary speaks to the belief that the energy of life and consciousness exists in all things. She is not alone in her beliefs. In Phenomenon of Man, a Catholic theologian, De Chardin, sets forth the idea that all things, even rocks, have an evolving consciousness. Mary suggests that all in life is energy, including thoughts.

Dr. Bezmen asks, "Mary can you shed some Light on Glastonbury Tor in what effects it has on humanity or individuals?

*   *   *

What I say to you know will be of great joy to your intellect and your heart but know that there is more.   Yeshua traveled far as we said, embracing many cultures and many beliefs, studying the mysticism of the world and the universe. Yes, he knew that everything on this planet was a living energy.   He knew it from the core of himself and taught us all the

The Teachings of Jesus

same.   We spoke to the trees, to the earth, and to the rocks. He laid upon his hands his thoughts and then into crystals and placed them not just there but wherever he traveled. Some of the writings that we refer to are not just what you would call a writing medium but are also placed in the living memory of the stones of the earth.

Indeed, there is a time capsule, there are many, and as the vibration of this planet increases and as the awareness starts to expand and grow many of you will be able to tap into, draw from the teachings and the information that lie there. No, you do not have to go to that site, for the knowledge and the wisdom are for all to have. It is a matter of raising the vibration and frequency of your thoughts and entering into the realm of Light that will bring the meaning and the information forward.   It will expand its energy and expand its fields as the awareness of the planet opens - as fear no longer has you by your hearts. As this planet lets go of fear so will go the anger and the rage. The expanded consciousness will begin to move in leaps and bounds uniting each one of us together once again.   Indeed there is going to be a great transition of this planet, not of death and destruction of life, but the death and destruction of fear and the rebirth of Light and truth. (E)

* * *

The Light of God Within

An idea that permeates all of Magdalene's messages is that positive change is in the power of LOVE and LIGHT. It is a real energy which can not only transform individual lives but all of humanity. It can lift them to a higher, more god-like place of life and consciousness.

*   *   *

Part of his words and teachings were that when you brought the Light of God into your humanity, if you could bring the Light into your life then into Light you shall return. If it is the darker, the heavier parts of humanity that you wish to hold onto, that you wish to clutch, then you shall get these again and again. Much of what is called karma is what you hold in highest esteem. Should you not hold life in esteem - yes, but life in humanity that you bring the Light of spirit into by loving your life, by working, by being and embracing the Divine within you.

You have the choice to remain in Light. It is all a choice. How many times did he bring that message to the people that he spoke to, to us who followed him? Was it not even during that last celebration together you refer to as supper that he said, "Take of this and drink for it is my blood - eat of it for it is my body."? So many ways this has been looked at, it has been interpreted, it has been understood and it has been misunderstood. Again, he was asking those who followed him to embrace within themselves the same Light that he carried and to acknowledge that what they had within them, their blood and their body was indeed a vessel of Divine Light, the Christed Light. It was not just the Light of one man but the Light of the cosmos, of the universe, of the all. This is the message I bring. Breath in, hold to your heart the spark of Divine Light that beats within you for the Light of God is in each one. And when you see the Light of God in your own eyes how easy to see it in each other. (G)

He and the others have come, so much of who they are, so many of their words; their thoughts and their love live in this room. With the others they connect with strands of Light as brilliant as shooting stars to the hearts of those who hold them dear. The time is drawing near for those to remember and to trust. Much time has gone by. We have come to you; we talk to you in your heart and in your sleep. You know your truth.   You remember so much and that which is not truth to you. You know and you see; discarding the words as you discard the husk from the wheat.   You hold the seeds in your hands as tenderly as any farmer. There are many of us here.   It is time to begin to sow the seeds once again, to remember, to never doubt or fear.

I asked him once of his divinity. He teases me now as he stands at my side challenging me to remember.   He had said the only difference between his divinity and ours is that he was sitting in the center of it, looking through it, around it, under it, above it, questioning it, embracing it, but never doubting it! And never fearing that the Light of God was a part of him and he was a part of the Light of God.   Many times I myself touched that. Thomas danced around it, embracing it when others did not see.   As I look toward that humanity and the humanity of all, the question, "Why do we fear the beauty of God's Love that is in us? Why do we not feel that which we are? Does a flower deny that it is a flower, does a tree deny that it is a tree?" And yet, we deny that we are a part of him and he is part of us. We deny at times that his words are alive in our thoughts; that we carry his seeds. Just like grains of sand being blown across the desert, each one a spark of the Divine. In touching the others we could feel the Divine within him. This is why we love the touch. It is not the touch of humanity that comforts us, it is the touch of life itself, and it is the touch of Light. It is the knowing, it is the remembering that comforts us the most.

I remember his eyes, but I remember his touch more; the touch that had the weight of the universe and yet was as Light as a feather. The touch that could move my hair without touching a strand, the touch that could hold my heart and never let it go. Each remember and know this, it was in the strength in being together that the Light shined so bright.

We were forced to flee, or were we? Had we stayed together could the Light have survived, would it have stayed and been as bright as it once was? From the time that he appeared to us a handful moved to Alexandria. That handful stands before you now. Joseph (of Arimathea), Yeshua's mother, myself, his wife; heavy with child and a child at her hand. Oh yes, there were others too. There were many others - we did not travel alone. Alexandria was a safe haven for us, but soon those that would see our words destroyed began to breathe at our backs. It was Joseph who said that we must go across the sea, that we journey by boat across the waters (to France).

It was there that we began again, moving, always moving. Always knowing that the Word must continue, always knowing that we would find each other again. It was not until the time of the parting of our bodies that we know that we would come lifetime after lifetime. It was not until the time of Light that we saw the destiny of that Light. So once again we gather and there are many. Once again our words fall upon your ears. Once again you are to choose your path. Once again you are asked to know the Light of the Divine within you and to bravely move forward with that Light and do not deny yourself.

Yes, we did deny him and I do say we, although I did not deny him. We were all connected to one another and alas, what one of my brothers had done also was done to me and through me. Nothing is separate and all is the same. This is one of his greatest teachings.

I have been asked of the dove that descended upon him at the time of his blessings in the water with John. It is written many times, by many men, of the dove that descended from the skies, the Spirit that moved around him, that hovered above him, that bestowed rays of Light around him for all that could see. Indeed, this dove did appear and indeed Light did shine on him and all that were present. It was the blessings of the Universe, it was blessings of God and all living things upon the vessel of this man that would speak the truth for so many and to those that would hear and would repeat those words. Indeed, he was prophesied by many before his coming and so were others. I dare say, even I was written about. The universe speaks; the voice of God speaks to all who will listen.

The words were written upon many scrolls and were kept for safety. Again I speak of these words and do not worry yourself to find them. Find them within the scrolls of your mind; find them written in the walls of your heart; find them in the vessels and the chambers of that which is so deep within you, for when you look there, you will find them. Words that may be familiar to you but understood in a different way. Wherever you look you can see his Light and his Love if you look through the eyes of the grace that dwells within you. There is no place inside of you that is unworthy of his love. (M)

*   *   *

Balancing of the Male and Female

There were many prophets who spoke before his birth, before his being in the flesh, of a time of a joining of the male and the female. Just words - but more than that, it was what you refer to as energy, life force, opposites that somehow fit together, a blend of all that man is within himself. Yeshua, represented the male energy to the men he spoke to because in that time, who else would they listen to. And they had a difficult time with him. Not your typical rabbi, nor was I your typical woman, but yet we knew of the balance, we knew of the peace that could stir within the hearts of every man and every woman. (C)

*   *   *

Trusting Your Heart

Someone says, "From everything that I have read about that time it didn't seem to me that Jesus, would have wanted to start another religion."

The Teachings of Jesus

*   *   *

And you see truth although not always accepted by all and difficult to embrace. It is humanity that has placed the wedge, the canyon between people. Those who follow the words of Yeshua if they look closely know that he came to unite the people, to bring together all people under one Light and one God. He did not destroy the Jews nor more did he create the Christian. He spoke of Light, he spoke of Love, he spoke of being compassionate to one another. No words were spoken to turn your backs on your fellow men. He spoke of no judgement, he spoke of joy. Would this be a man that would say, "Only I have truth."? Indeed, find comfort in what you know in your heart and do not try to prove it to others. Just be, just be in your Light and in your Love and bring your Light into life. Do not struggle, rejoice for you have found the truth you seek and it has not come from me but from your heart.

*   *   *

Laying on of Hands

Much of what has fascinated believers for the past two thousand years was Jesus' power to heal the physical and mental ailments of those he touched.

*   *   *

The laying on of the hands is something that is well written of and referred to as miracles. The word miracle had no meaning in our language and in our time. There were healings. The Divine Light and Love flowed through each one of us. We followed the ways of Yeshua as he taught us all what we were capable of. We watched and we learned and we did as he told us to and there were many healings, not merely of the body but also that of the soul. (D)

Throughout the world there were many cultures, many peoples, that you would refer to as primitive, who used their hearts and connected to the earth that they were part of, and drew in the energy and the love around them to create change. They knew how to open their minds as we were learning to open, once again, that which we had forgotten about.   Yesh helped us open to those things, he taught us as he learned also the ways of many, the ways of laying on hands, of helping those to open to themselves. (B)

*   *   *

Look Within Eyes

Mary of Bethany speaks

*   *   *

And he knew the women all by name.   And when they were working among the crowds there was a wonderful thing that used to happen.   One of them, one of us, would turn around and look down the hillside or across the courtyard and catch his eye and there was a heart connection that went out between him and us.   And anyone who walked through that at that moment was healed.   It was really beautiful and it happened all the time.   Whenever he made a heart connection with whomever he looked at of those incredible women that traveled with him all the time, healing took place. (B)

*   *   *

Connectedness of All Souls

In addition to the energy of Light and LOVE

that Jesus taught was the idea of connectedness of all life and, most useful to spiritual development, the connectedness of humanity.

* * *

Many lessons, many teachings were not understood during those times. There were those that could embrace what was being said. The essence of life itself, the life force, the higher part of our being could be sensed and felt. He would raise his consciousness, his vibrations, for he was an ascended one who could easily expand to all that he was all and that we all are. To be in his presence was to feel that essence and know it.

His teachings were to not judge each other so harshly. So much of what he taught was of the consciousness of all souls and all beings. He wanted us to know that each one of our thoughts affected another; that we were all connected by magnificent Light. (He referred to us as threads of Light. This held us and wove us together in unity.) To judge another was to judge oneself and that no one act was more terrible than another and that the greatest act of all was that of compassion and love and once we stepped into compassion, once we raised into the essence of love itself, all would be understood. It is very difficult to embrace that now. It was even more difficult then. Everything was seen as good or evil. It was his essence and his Light that created the spaces in between that connected it all to the one. (F)

* * *

Lifting Consciousness

Accepting the idea of this connectedness, because we come from the same God source, lays the foundation for humanity to grow in spiritual development through the raising of our consciousness. In fact, it is this elevation of consciousness that is what has been referred to as the Second Coming.

Dr. Bezmen asks, "History has shown that most of the power has been given to men at the expense of women. Is this going to change?"

*   *   *

Yes.   When the man is willing is to accept all that he is and all the gifts of the female within him. When he does not fear to create the balance inside he will no longer need to control.

It is lifting that consciousness.   All one can do to create that change is to hold the truth in your own heart.   As each one elevates to that consciousness, the one that he spoke of, the one that he taught, it will be felt by those around you, it will ripple through the universe, one vibration touching another.   You can not create change in those who can not see.   They must see themselves.

You must be in your own truth and know all aspects, of who you are and embrace them.   Those around you will see it even if they don't understand it. Your vibration will create a tide throughout the sea of humanity, the sea of humanity will move in the direction of Light for the cycle must come full circle and that which we are we will return again.   Know this to be truth. (F)

The Teachings of Jesus

* * *

Raising Vibrations

* * *

It is the connection of each one that will bring the peace that is looked for. You asked before about those who are not raised to that frequency, that vibration, see them as those I just spoke of that will continue to walk in fear not knowing their Light. If you doubt the Light within you look to someone who sees it in you. Draw upon their Light to brighten yours. Those that are present here will rise into the consciousness of Light, it has already begun. (F)

* * *

Be Without Judgement

If one accepts that all of humanity is connected, not just biologically, but in spirit and consciousness as well, the problem of judgement is certainly diminished, if not eliminated. Most of the seeds of man's problems, from personal relationships to world wars begin with judgement. Our capacity for hurtful actions, both personally and internationally, is rooted in this judgement.

* * *

Dear one, trust with your heart, trust with your vision of what you have within you of that magnificent Light that will illuminate truth before you, that will guide you ever homeward and on your way. It is difficult to remain in spirit while in humanity but this is your greatest gift connecting to your spirit and living it through your humanity. It is a gift that has been given. It is the gift that Yeshua, Buddha, Mohammed and many others tried to bring to light?

You need not step aside your body and your mind but honor it. How else will you interpret your visions if not through the mind that was given you? Falling from spirit is what you allude to, many fearing that they fall out of the grace of God when they despair, when they experience their humanity. This is the time to cherish and honor the spirit within. It is the time that draws us to spirit and should not draw us away from it. It is the time for reaching, for not falling away, for in spirit there is comfort. That which you feel to be your shortcomings are just steps along the way. Be without judgement. The words he spoke so many times, "Be without judgement" of self. This is where it begins. (C)

* * *

Someone asks about achieving non-judgement.
* * *

A difficult task for most and you are not the only one who carries this thought but one who is willing to speak it. It is not with effort that this will happen. Imagine yourself lying in a field with the sky above you and the earth around you and in that quiet moment feel the awe and in that awe there is no judgement. It is a choice of letting go of that which stands between you and your joy. It is like holding a heavy tablet of stone and saying, "My friend this tablet is so heavy it hurts my hand." Put it down, rest and do not struggle with it. Perhaps you do not need to carry that stone.

It is so difficult, we make things difficult for

ourselves. This has not changed, always taking the harder path when one lays so easily near, when judging yourself, condemning yourself, in anything but love. Think of one that you know, that you've seen, that you've heard of who has done something that you judge far worse and then look at them with the eyes of love and compassion. It is easy to do for most. And then look with compassion at yourself and know that all that lies within you is the Light, the Light of the Truth and that all that you judge to be less than you are is merely baggage, merely layers and veils of cloth that you can shed. Ask yourself, "Why do I hold onto what holds me back, what burdens me?" If you were warm would you not take off your cloak? Lay it aside and look to the heavens above you to the Light above you, or to the eyes of one who has loved you and allow that to enter and fill all those spaces where doubt and fear dwell. Imagine yourself to be without flaw and love that image, for in loving that image in truth you love who you are, the essence of who you are. You all aspire to be the Light which already exists. (C)

*　*　*

Find Joy and Stop Suffering

*　*　*

And it is not in the plan of God and was not asked by the Light of God to suffer. It is not just in this religion but in other cultures and faiths of humanity. More people in the name of God took upon themselves unnatural, very unnatural habits and lifestyles, seeing themselves as sacrificing their humanity for God. God did not want you to sacrifice your humanity - this is what Yeshua brought. He wanted you to be in joy; the Light of God wants you to find your truth and your happiness. He does not want you to suffer, but instead, to use the Light to find the joy and to stop the suffering. Why do we make it so hard - when the Light was to make things easier for us. (E)

*   *   *

What Happens to Those Who Do Not Accept the Light?

In some of our religious teachings, a judging God is depicted. Whole peoples have been destroyed by the God of the Old Testament. In Christ's name wars have been waged and millions killed. At the personal level Mary was asked about what happens to those who will not accept the teachings of Jesus.

Dr. Bezmen asks, "In those people who will not accept the Light, what will happen to those people?"

*   *   *

It will not be as some have said; they will not be cast upon rocks, tortured in flames, beaten into submission. They will merely be in the dense energy of the human plane, walking through life empty as many do now, not much different than the masses of humanity have done since the beginning of time, using only what they can see and what can be proven to them. They just will never raise to the consciousness that is available to them but will always have the choice to do so. They will not be banished into a world where now they have lost the opportunity. It will always be there for their soul, lifetime after lifetime, or they may embrace it now. The choice is theirs. (F)

CHAPTER TEN

Magdalene's Insights

"Pray in the words you need to pray in, it does not matter. Think it in any language, feel it in any ritual that gives comfort to your soul. Light is Light, and when it's on it will fill you."

Much of the channeling of Mary gives us infor-mation about the time and life of Jesus and those that followed him. Not only was Mary a close confidant of Jesus but she was left, as were the others, to carry on without his physical presence. When the teacher leaves, the student must step forward and become the teacher or what was taught is lost. The concepts have to be absorbed and reworked into language each spirit can understand. When this process is successful, a true integration and understanding happens. There are many places in the channeling sessions where Mary demonstrates just such an integration of concepts. In addition, because time has passed and she is of spirit, the power of her messages might be even greater now than they were when she walked the earth with Jesus. Certainly, she presents a larger perspective than we have had before. She speaks with the authority of one who knows as she speaks of consciousness and former incarnations.

Consciousness is Eternal

Dr. Bezmen asks, "You seem to be saying that what belief you take into transition, what you expect, is what you will get and that the moment you ask for higher wisdom it will be there for you. Is it the same, both in spirit and in the flesh?"

* * *

Always. There is no difference. Consciousness is eternal, the forms that it takes, the shapes that it takes, the senses that it uses does not change the essence of what it is. You are correct and many are following that path. The consciousness of God, of

Source, of Universe, by many names, by many sculptors, all ask of you to embrace the same thing, the self as perfect and whole. Experiencing, feeling, learning, growing, understanding, loving, sharing - do it all and do it from a place of joy. (L)

*   *   *

Sparks of Parallel Times

*   *   *

Indeed, the memories of times gone by, the strength of the messages then and now, are timeless. They are even now more powerful than before. The time of two thousand years gone by was a time of great fear. Parallels between lifetimes are strong and a message for all. The doubt to know who was friend, who was foe, not knowing who we could trust for safe harbor, not knowing whose hands to put our lives in, and his words. This has not changed and it has shown itself even now. Do you not ask the same questions?

At that time, many of the men gathered as your leaders are gathering now, deciding what to do with those that betrayed him, those that were his enemies. Do they not even argue now who the enemy was? Who caused such pain and confusion?   The men argued, many continued to argue throughout their lives, plotted revenge, killed in his name!   Others walked the path, walked on the road, journeyed far into uncharted waters.   They walked through the fear, as you must now, pushed past the grief and the anger and stepped into the unknown. We walked with his words of love not knowing if our fate would be as his, not knowing who would betray us, murder us in our sleep or offer us the safety of their homes. It was a time of uncertainty as it is now.

Myself, and many of the women, chose to walk in that Love. This is not to belittle the men. There were men who walked with us, those that were not caught in their own rage and fear. We chose to leave that behind. What better time to remember walking that path? Did we protect ourselves? Yes, we did. Did we open our hearts to feel what must be right? We did. Did we look for the truth in the eyes and the hearts of those that we met? We did. Did we find shelter from our enemies? Yes. But it was not in fear that we gathered. In those places unseen by the enemies, those that were filled with hate, those who did not understand, we did not dwell in them.

We spoke of stories; we would laugh and cry at his words, at experiences that we had remembering his smile, his eyes. We would lay our hands on one another. By doing so the flame was tended. We kept the embers of his love and the love for one another and for all men alive. We taught our children not to hate the enemy or to fear but to keep their hearts open as we sheltered them and protected them as best we could. Things do not have to change and have not changed. The universal Light of God asks you now to choose a path as we were asked to choose then. Many followed me without knowing why. Joseph of Arimathea and I were considered quite insane at times. Moving on, forging through rock and bramble, singing, praying always remembering the truth of the Light and the power of Love.

The moment I would release even a little bit, pain, anger, and grief would begin to flood in. Whenever I allowed my Light to dim, the gates would open to let in the sorrow. I would have to turn the Light on brighter and it was not easy.   And when my Light would not shine there were others around me who would Light it, who would touch my heart, who would look into my eyes, who would hold me in their arms and I would feel him again.   We embrace each other now, brother and sisters of Light, it is not the Light of Christianity, or the Light of Buddha, nor the Light of Abraham, it is the Light of the Highest of the High and express it as you would.

Pray in the words you need to pray in, it does not matter. Think it in any language, feel it in any ritual that gives comfort to your soul. Light is Light, and when it's on it will fill you.   Love is powerful and true and any master teacher in any time knows this to be truth and you will always have comfort even in the darkest hours. (O)

*   *   *

The Path is Most Important

*   *   *

It is not the path that is unclear to you.   It is your destination.   This is what remains unknown. The path that you are on is indeed one of your heart. Be present with it, follow each voice that rises within you, and ask of each day in the quietness, in the stillness, in the radiant love and peace. Ask that each day brings to you that awareness, that it brings to you the lessons, that it brings to you the way that you seek.   If our minds are focused on that place that we want to go to we miss so much.

Yeshua spoke to us once of a long journey.   He spoke of when our people walked a very long path look-

ing for the promise of peace in the land of God.   Had
they not looked at each step they were taking they
would have missed that which was given to them.
They would have missed all the opportunities to learn
and to grow so that when they reached their destination they would have all that they needed.   It is as
though the Light of God leaves little gifts along the
way, leaves us gentle offerings.   Think of going on a
journey, that in the destination you will need certain
things to open the final door. As you walk your path, if
you are looking only at the door you are to open, you
may miss the key that lies on the side of the road. You
may miss the turn in the road that leads you to the
door that is yours.   You may follow one who walks
before you to their door instead of your own. You may
end up walking the path of another instead of the path
of your soul. It is not an easy answer that I give you,
frustrating it can be, and many times we were frustrated by his words.

We wanted answers, "Rabbi, if you are of God
why can you not tell us what to do?" He would smile
that smile and I knew what was coming, as the words
would fall from my mouth.   The answers would be
found within me. It is enough to know that as you follow the truth of your heart, if your intent is to be connected to the spirit of Light within you to guide you
through your humanity, through your purpose, so it
will be.

Each day, each step will unfold for you.   Your
humanity is creating that path and that journey. You
are laying the bricks, the spirit is the mortar that is
holding them together, that makes your path sound
and strong, that keeps your feet steadfast on the earth.

And yes, you did know me.   It is enough said. (J)

* * *

Views on Women

There is much evidence in the sessions that Mary was never an "average" woman. Certainly, meeting and following Jesus did much to influence her understanding of the flawed views of the male dominated society.

Dr. Bezmen asks, "How is it that women who bring our children into the world physically have lost so much status and are treated so badly in our world today?

* * *

This I can answer for you. In the beginning of time, when we took the shape of our humanity as we know it now, there was a splitting, a separation of the Light beings and that which would be female.   That split would hold the essence of what is female and was given the duty, the gift, the joy, of bringing forth life in a very obvious way.   And this was known, at first, during the time of our higher frequency and women were treated as equally as men.   There was a time when male and female saw in each other all of that which was glory and wonder.

When we began to procreate, the essence of life that came from the man was known and understood and held in the same esteem as the life that came forth from the woman, not one more important than the other.   Everything was done in balance, there was no struggle.   There was a knowing, there was a drawing upon the strengths and the qualities of one another to bring together those two parts of the essence of our being as a whole. So male and female worked together, side by side, together much stronger than each one separately.

Soon, as we moved further in our development, as we journeyed from Light and descended into the denser parts of our humanity, as the darkness fell upon us and the time of forgetting began, we saw each other as different. That which was in awe of female and her ability to give life, to bring forth life. That which was in awe of the strength of the woman to know, to heal, to carry life was overshadowed by the strength and physical force of that which was male. He felt powerless in the beginnings for it was she who brought forth the life of the child. It was she who knew what should be eaten and how to heal with herbs and that of the earth. He depended on her for healing, for comfort, for medicine. Power began, struggle for power began. He, forgetting that he had life within him and forgetting that he too had the gifts of knowing but chose not to use them. It was the male energy that got caught in the quest for power and so it began.

In the beginning, that which was called prophet in the early times of the tribes during the time of Abraham, it was the men who brought forth the messages and marched forward. In truth, the women were receiving the same knowledge, being guided the same way. When women began to speak forth, the men feared once again women's power. Man gave the women their silence. It became law that women were not to be spoken to in public. It became law by those men saying that they spoke the words of God that women should not be taught. It was also during this time that women who followed messages were considered sorcerers, were considered to have magical powers. Indeed, some women did use those powers incorrectly. It was not uncommon for a woman to poison her husband. It is very complex. The power struggle went back and forth.

The rules known as religions, the boundaries beginning, separating two parts of a whole even further until Yeshua. Until he spoke of this. Men were not the only ones that were "evil". I do not make light of this matter, these words in this manner, for many women indeed also abused the power that they had, perpetuating the fear. Balance was coming back once again, his words being heard, spoken in a way that was understood by all, well maybe not all. For even those men who followed had difficulty with accepting women for the laws were long and drummed into their hearts. After he was gone, women rose once again and once again were halted. The time is coming now, much talk in your universe of understanding that male and female, man and woman stand in each soul and you can draw upon their strengths within you, as was asked, as the vibration as we elevate back into the consciousness, back into the essence of Light the balance will return, in truth it has already begun. (F)

* * *

Male - Female Role Model

Dr. Bezmen states, "Today, when there is so much confusion between the male and female within each of us, and the male and female in our society, you

*stand as an incredible role model. I think that the men
of our time will do well to learn from you.*

*　*　*

I can not take credit for what lies within each
one. I was blessed to be in his presence and in his love.
I was blessed to see the Light in his eyes and see my
own Light reflected back as though I was looking into a
pool of clear water. I was blessed to see myself as he
saw me. I was blessed to be received by his humanity
as friend. I was blessed to have the wisdom of listening
to the mind of my heart and not of my head for if I had
I would not have followed! If I had listened to the
teachings in my mind that were given to me as a child
and held them as gospel truth, if I held them firmly as
though written in stone unchangeable, inflexible, I
could not have learned what I did.

Balance of male and female as you speak, I
guess that could be said for we did challenge one
another. Many do not see him as the man that he was.
Many words spoken, God and man, as each one of you
are, but yet he was viewed more as the God and less as
the man. His humanity was quick, charming. He
could be angered, he could be tested, frustrated,
annoyed. He could be clever, always with open arms
to those who came, always able to reach into that Light
and bring from it a strength that embraced so many.
Yes, there were many of us, and many of us bring
many different messages of Light, of healing, of raising
consciousness and raising the vibration of the universe. (G)

*　*　*

CHAPTER ELEVEN

Writings

"There are those that wish to believe that the same man that they refer to as the Son of God was illiterate and did not write or read. Yeshua wrote as well as we all did; journaling our times, experiences, lessons and in great detail, now to be lost...to be lost, to be hidden...to be distorted."

Some are familiar with the unearthing of the Dead Sea Scrolls and the writings from the library at Nag Hammadi. These ancient writings have challenged the beliefs of Christianity and Judaism, sometimes reinforcing those beliefs and sometimes contradicting them. The uncovering of ancient writings began long before the Dead Sea Scrolls were found and continues as an ongoing process. The fact that this information was written thousands of years ago does not guarantee its veracity. It was written by humans who, like all of us, rarely see or communicate without distortion. Yet writings, and particularly ancient writings, are important to us because they are tangible and therefore add the power of physical evidence to our beliefs. Writings are what can be left behind in the earthly realm when the spirit leaves.

Choices

*   *   *

It was a choice of my soul to leave when it did but in my humanity it was despair and great sadness of my heart and not at just the loss of a dear friend for that was understood. It was despair of watching that which we worked for so hard to be altered in so many ways, that which we sought to unite being divided and the division becoming greater and greater. Instead of uniting under one Light of the Divine God many more divisions were made in the name of God and in the name of Christ. Much interpretation of what he said was changed, his writings lost, hidden, altered. Truth changed hand to hand, mouth to mouth, ear to ear until no longer did the simple truth stand. (G)

*   *   *

All the Apostles Wrote

Mary of Bethany gives us an overview of the importance of writings of Jesus and his followers and how much material was written.

* * *

All the apostles wrote, Yeshua wrote, Mary the Magdalene wrote. There were other women who were educated who wrote. Anything that had to do with his humanness was gradually stricken from the record. And so the whole thing has died and it died very, very quickly. There are writings that still exist. There have been gospels that have been discovered similar to the Dead Sea Scrolls and more will be discovered in the next few years and his humanness will begin to emerge. His writings were preserved. They were taken, by his children out of that land where they really were not welcome and they were taken to what you now call England and dispersed from there to Ireland, to France and eventually even across the sea to the eastern coast of this country.

They will be discovered, and they will be discovered in your lifetime and the truth will come out. We must realize that humans are humans. The people that edited his writings and all the other writings were not malicious; they were just trying to protect whatever their interest was at the time, whatever they thought was right. But as it was done, much was lost and there is purpose in that.

* * *

But now it has come full circle and the real truth about what happened then and who he was will

come out because people are ready to hear it now when
they were not a long time ago. (B)

* * *

Many Followers Wrote

*The Magdalene mentions in several channeling
sessions that there were many who wrote.*

* * *

We are only fractions of what happened, a collection of ideas and memories written by those who followed.   There were many more who wrote including
Yesh, including myself, of our experiences and our life
during those years and times.   It was chosen by the
church that certain writings would be eliminated. (B)

There are many writings of the many who followed.   Many writings of Yesh, every detail was
recorded, every moment was treasured.   They were
not thought important at the time just merely daily
events, diaries of feelings, of emotions, of relationships
between people.   There were many stories, the ones
that were chosen, sought out, were just examples of
parts of times of his life, and of ours.   Yes the writings
will be known.   They will be known. (B)

More the teachings, more the writings of
Yeshua, the writings of Peter, Phillip, Thomas and
myself soon to be uncovered.   These jars just keep
showing up. (C)

* * *

Two ideas about the writings surfaced during the channeling sessions. First, the documents we have of Jesus, his message, and his followers are in bits and pieces, and some of it is humanly flawed in its accuracy. The other idea, is that writings exist which have been hidden from us.

* * *

The writings of Yeshua, of his wife, of many of his followers, of his children, of his brothers and his sisters do exist and there are many copies that circulate even now. Bits and pieces, yes, and many times the words have been changed the same way a stone changes as it rolls down a hill losing and gaining, losing and gaining again. (I)

So much was not understood and so much was written by all of us and I tell you now that those writings still do exist in your time. They are present. There are those that wish to believe that the same man that they refer to as the son of God was illiterate and did not write or read. Yeshua wrote, as we all did, journaling our times, our experiences, our lessons in great detail only to be lost, to be hidden, and to be distorted.

Much of what is written that you have available to you now is part of truth but I ask you to look at what you read, what you hear and then understand that it was different languaging then, many dialects, many languages, many interpretations of those words. Some things were not meant to be distorted, it was not the intent to distort, but in the translating much was lost, much was misunderstood.

Then there were those writings that were very carefully deleted. Words that had no use to those who would write them vanished from the pages. But I tell you that these words are available to you in your heart and in your wisdoms. Call upon the Light within you and ask what is truth; you will not be misled. And this man, this Rabbi that I follow cannot lead to any place other than to truth. He knew no other way. (B)

*   *   *

Editing Transformed Magdalene's Role

*   *   *

Everything is, as it should happen. This is hard to understand but even out of this many good things have risen. There were those that found their joy in living the Word of God. Yes, indeed, there are many misconceptions in the teachings, even in the teachings of my life as you have spoken of. I was indeed sainted, held in esteem, until a parable was needed and a lesson was needed and I was the first name to come to the mouth of the man who spoke it. In one word, in one sentence, in one moment, history was indeed changed. This is just a small sample of what has occurred through time but not just in religion for humanity has freedom of will, of choice, and it is this you are subject to. But it is also this that you can free yourself from by learning your own truth. (B)

*   *   *

Gnostic Writings

* * *

Gnostic pages have been uncovered before and indeed, yes, more have been revealed. The topic of writings tends to frequent your humanity. There are many writings that are coming, words written on parchment as validation of what you already perceived that may have been and what will be. And in your humanity, indeed, there is a part of you that needs this and this is understood.

But I tell you, as sure as the Light of the Universe is eternal, that the words that you seek and the knowledge you look for you already have. Indeed, more pages have been found, caves have always provided wondrous hiding places and places of storage. Our earth has provided those places for us, vaults for that which we, in humanity, wish to protect. But our souls have etched in the facets of our Light these writings as well as the writings of Yeshua, myself and others, the writings of some of you who sit in this room will be revealed and in your lifetime. (F)

* * *

Hiding the Writings

* * *

It did not serve the purpose of a patriarchal society to have my writings hanging about. About the Gospel of Thomas, they were so despondent because they knew that these writings contained information about the quality of man and woman, their quality of Light, the abolishment of barriers of class between people. We watched the writings be preserved after the writers went into Light with the others and rejoiced as they were placed in safe keeping and were saddened when the eyes that fell upon the writings did what they may with them. Even in these jars most of these writings have been put aside. It is fascinating and human nature. The part of the experience was that although the writings were not wanted they were not destroyed. What kept the hands of these men from destroying the writings that they feared? Why did they wrap them, maintain them and hide them away. Was the Light within them still guiding them even though their minds chose differently? Was there a greater force, a Light that drove them to maintain and preserve that which they feared?

As you grow in Light and as the information is revealed the answers you seek will be answered. (C)

There are those of you who surround me now that know what these lost writings are. There are those of you present who may choose to remember or wait to be told. So beautiful are the words that will be spoken for they came from a pure heart, but a human one. For when we take form and choose a lifetime to be present we embrace it fully, that human experience, with all its pains, with all its joys and with all its passions. He was no exception to that nor were any of the great prophets. Understand the humanity, connect it to your own, and then see the Light within that resided in them - there is no difference. (A)

* * *

Rumors of Uncovered Writings

Dr. Bezmen asked, "Recently a student of ours has gone to Scotland and there is talk there of a church that is believed to be a new hot spot and there might be some writings of Yeshua in the walls. Is there anything that you could share about that?"

* * *

The part of the earth that they seek these messages does indeed hold some truth but not only this place. There are many places on your planet that hold these words and these truths, some written by his hand others written by other masters of Light and those connected to them. This place that they speak of now indeed has messages within its walls but they are not written in the hand of the one known as Yeshua, but are written of him by one who was close to him. Much of it is written, some of it is his humanity and what he felt of it. It must not be taken word for word but felt with.

* * *

Dr. Bezmen asks,"Is that writings of John?" and Mary Magdalene responds.

* * *

Do you not already know? (F)

* * *

Dr. Bezmen continues, "Mary, we've heard that the writings of Jesus should be unearthed close to this time and I also received a reading about ten years ago that talked about this as well. Can you give us any new information about whether they have been discovered or unearthed?"

* * *

What I can bring to you now is that some of these writings are in the hands of man. Interesting enough, humanity has not changed in two thousand years, for what they hold in their own hands they do not recognize for what it is. They are still struggling with what they have found and they have not found all of it for his writings are not in one place.

He did much traveling. Yeshua was not good at keeping things together. It was his humanity. We teased him endlessly, "Light of God shining through his eyes and he couldn't keep his belongings together." He would often, in haste, in his joy, get caught in his words and with the people and become easily distracted. If someone called his name his eyes went to them immediately and what he was doing was left. There are writings he left, parables, stories that he wrote, some left deliberately, given as gifts, in Egypt, in India, in the places that you call England, Ireland. The writings are starting to be found and those that are finding them do not realize what they have. Soon, within the next year of your time, one man will know clearly what he has in his hands and it will change all that is known. Many of your religions will be shaking from their very roots, shaken the way the cypress would move in the wind, desperately clutching the rocks to hold on to what they thought was truth. It is coming.

* * *

Dr. Bezmen asks, "Mary do we have any information about that at this time? Are these new truths that are just brand new to humanity or are they things that have been taught by some, understood by some, but now maybe on a grander scale?"

* * *

Because the wisdoms of the universe are open to all, those who have connected to the Christ consciousness and to the universal Light and brought it into their heart have access to what was written. So it is available to many and to many the enlightenment has already begun. Yes, there are some stories that will be validated by this writing. His stories and his letters about his wife will shake your religious world to its core for it is one thing to have theory of something and another to have the words in your hand that describe the love that he had for Bethany. Much will have to change, for those things that people once knew, as their truth will begin to dissolve in their very hands.

It is a lesson not to clutch tightly to anything but to always be open to the possibilities of the all. It will be less shocking to those that have opened their awareness and trusted and felt what might be truth. For those it will be a validation, a sigh of joy and relief. " Yes it is as I have thought, as I felt, as I believed in my heart." For others quite a task. The same task we were faced with as we brought the Word of God around to those that were not quite ready to hear. You can imagine the councils of the highest rabbis as I would walk into a room and say, "I want to speak to you of this man Jesus, the one who now dwells with his father, my father. It is time that you hear his truth," and I was escorted out, and I would enter another way. It was not for the weak or the soft willed woman of our days to bring forth the truth nor is it now. It is not superiority but an equality that must be felt and known between man and woman.   When this balance is known, so will the truth be known.   All of these things of the universe are coming into alignment now.

The vibration of Light is increasing the vibration of your planet, your world.   Your universe is changing around you and more of you are enlightening, are opening your awareness to truth. Now is the time to embrace, as it was at the time that he came.   The universe, the energy is in the same alignment that it is now. Then was the time of the awakening and so again it is now.   What will you do with it this time?   What will your truth be?

*   *   *

Dr. Bezmen asks, "Is there anything more you could tell us about any of the particulars about where the writings will come out?   I have a more specific question.   We keep getting in our meditations that there is a cave in Ireland containing some writings in a jar sealed with wax.   Is the cave that we are led to owned by the family of a woman that we know?"

*   *   *

There is more than one place that writings dwell.   Yes indeed, there is a cave that contains some of the writings.   They are intact, but there are many other places where writings exist, buried in walls in what you refer to as churches, monasteries, chapels, holy places.   There are many places that these writing exist, there are those who hold the writings and do not know whose words they are, for he did not begin his writings with, "I am Yeshua and here is what I have to say."   They are the words of a man .   It will be up to those who read them to feel with the words and to hear them within, to know for where they came.   There will be passages, references made of some of those figures that you know as being in his presence but there were many that were with him, names that you are not familiar with.

I must say there is a sketching of the likeness of Yeshua and some of us that you refer to in your humanity at this time as the Last Supper. I say to you that that room was very crowded and they were not the only ones in that room, nor was there a neat table laid out so elegantly. It would have been nice but the truth be known we had Passover in a very small humble building on the second story of a dwelling and many of us crowded into this space to celebrate this time. Yes, he was there and yes, we surrounded him, elbow to elbow, shoulder to shoulder, hot, dusty, not at all what you would consider pleasant.   But then he spoke and as he spoke many in the room wrote his words.   Each one writing what they felt they were hearing, writing what they saw, or what they perceived to see. Passover it was and to celebrate in memory of him it was to be done.   Where has that gone?   The writings will come; the first ones will come from the area known as Egypt, these will be the first to be found, to be interpreted as the words of a man named Yeshua.   That is all I can say at this time.

* * *

Dr. Bezmen asks, "Does the Vatican have any of those writings, and if so, do they know what they have? Are they intentionally holding back information?"

* * *

Yes. There are writings that did not support the patriarchal society of the religious movement of that time. Yes, I do say unto you that they have these writings, writings of many who walked the earth with Yeshua.

* * *

Dr. Bezmen asks, "Including your writings?"

* * *

Yes. But they will not be able to contain them very much longer. Consciousness is raising even in these places. They will not be able to withhold the truth.

* * *

Looking for further clarification Dr. Bezmen asks, "Are you saying that every one of those popes knew about that and are deliberately holding back this information? You mean to tell me that they know this is the truth and they are not teaching truth?"

* * *

I say to you that some of what they have is known to them and that decisions have been made by more than one person that to bring forth some of what was found and some of what has been interpreted would bring chaos to a religious system. And the choice not to share some of this information is not out of malice, at least in their thinking, but of fear of the chaos of those things that have been held in ritual belief, the belief that there needs to be boundaries, the belief that there needs to be control. For some of this to come forward would bring chaos to all that they know.

* * *

Dr. Bezmen asks, "Can you share what form they are in? Are they in the form of scrolls?"

* * *

They are written in scrolls. They are in your humanity, tangible. They can be read, they can be held, they can be touched. The truth is written. The messages are recorded. They are known. They are feared.

* * *

Dr. Bezmen inquires, "Will we become privileged to that information?"

* * *

It begins first with the privilege of knowing and hearing it within your own heart. You do not need to lay eyes on this to know it. You can turn to your hearts and dare to open the doors of the memories and to hear the words yourself, the words you spoke, the words you heard, the words you wrote. There are even those here present, who walked lifetimes soon after his, that read the true words. Indeed, that which has never made sense (to you), today is, because you know different and always have. But these writings have been seen and some have been said and some have been discarded and in this lifetime some will be brought forward to satisfy your humanity. (J)

* * *

Hidden Information Surfacing as Memories

* * *

Humanity wants the answers to be brought to them. When it is time to remember it will come and be known to you. Your name already is in your heart and

in your mind.   Each one of your souls has memories of
the journeys you have taken.   Each one of your souls
has that which holds the visions of one who has walked
before.   Upon death, you join the Light of God and you
join the memories of all.

When you come into this humanity you bring
with you many of those thoughts, many of those
visions, many of those words.   You have chosen to
bring them forward in this lifetime to understand
humanity in a different way.   Indeed, many sitting
before me know that their connection to Yeshua was
more than what they were taught as a child.   Many
have memory; it stirs within them yet eagerly dismissed by the conscious mind, "This can not possibly be
true!"

For those of you that have memories, that feel
and somehow know that you stood before him and felt
his smile and his eyes and his touch and his love; is it
doubt and unworthiness that does not allow that door
to swing open for you to step in?   Look into your heart
and see which doors are closed. Begin, begin to look
now.   Begin to feel what it is you already know. (J)

*   *   *

Teachings Were Changed

*When truth passes from one human to another,
it changes slightly. As it continues to be passed again
and again, the deviation from the original becomes even
greater.   When we are trying to understand the teachings of Jesus, these changes become all important.*

How close is our understanding of his teachings to what he actually wanted us to know? Mary gives us some insight.

* * *

The words did not appear the way they do now and the words traveled from one mouth to another. Needless to say they changed meaning many times, adding to the confusion of what was the truth. Even what is written was written in the truth of that hand that wrote it. What tools do you need? How do you get through these times? Trust with your heart, trust with the vision of what you have within you of that magnificent Light that will illuminate truth before you, that will guide you ever homeward and along your way. It is difficult to remain in spirit, while in humanity, but this is your greatest gift. Connecting to your spirit and living it through your humanity is a gift that has been given. (C)

* * *

Information Was Destroyed

* * *

All that know the name of Yeshua know him to be Rabbi, know him to be one of the faithful Jews of Israel, one of the faithful teachers and followers of God. This is spoken of in the writings of Judaism as well as in the writings of Christianity and many other writings. What happens to truth and to words as they pass from humanity to humanity and when in humanity each soul has the ability, the right of interpreting their own truth. Ego, power and seeking truth in things other than the Light has brought very many men to crimes, to acts of unthinkable horror.

Although the hiding and destroying of information, of writings, is not considered a crime by most, it did stop the information from passing from mind to mind. However the Light that has its place in all men has access to that information. (C)

*   *   *

Egos Edit Truth

*   *   *

Christianity did not stop the fighting, the ego and the distortion of truth: that which it set to change. Those who established a difference from Judaism created their own havoc; their own egos, their own crimes of hiding truth.   Look at what is referred to as Crusades.   Were there any greater crimes spoken in the name of God, of Light, created by men seeking power.   In their truth, they sought the power of God and had faith, in truth, that they were walking the path of God.   I do not condemn them but it is a lesson for humanity. (C)

*   *   *

CHAPTER TWELVE

The Passion

"He did not want to die in that manner, his humanity did not ask for it but he allowed his humanity and the humanity of man around him to unfold the way it would, not controlling the thoughts of other men."

If one had to list those events in Jesus' life central to the Christian faith certainly the crucifixion and resurrection would be near the top. To believers Jesus demonstrated with his very life the surety of the eternalness of life in spirit. A question often asked, even by the scoffers at the cross is, "How could a loving Father/God allow his child to suffer the pain and humiliation of the cross?" Mary was asked this very question.

Why Did God Allow the Crucifixion?

*   *   *

It is still the understandings of humanity that death is a punishment, that pain is a punishment. Looking at everything as good or bad, judging everything from the perspective of humanity. Yeshua, his spirit, his soul, his Light, knew of his destiny far before his coming to this earth, to this plane, not remembering it when he was born a child but having visions of it as he grew older. He did not want to die in that manner, his humanity did not ask for it but he allowed his humanity and the humanity of man around him to unfold the way it would, not controlling the thoughts of other men. It was never the purpose of Light and of Truth to control the actions of man. It is of free will that we come and of free will we are given and part of that free will led to the events of his death.

Was it necessary to die that way? Even I think not and question that and was angered by that and was sorrowed by that along with the others. But looking through the span of time, would his name be remembered when others who had spoken the same words as he are not known to you? Hundreds of thousands have spoken those words and you do not know them. Was it necessary? Perhaps, but he was taken from pain the moment he surrendered his soul to the Light of his father. Many have been saved and many have been lost in the name of God. He directed those to whom he spoke to embrace their own Light and find their own truth; what greater gift can we have? (C)

* * *

The Last Supper

Our understanding of the Last Supper is either imagined from reading the Biblical text or from viewing what artists have painted many hundreds of years after the event. Mary Magdalene and Mary of Bethany give us new insight into this event and the symbolism of bread and wine as flesh and blood.

Mary of Bethany states....

* * *

In terms of the Last Supper we were there.

* * *

The Magdalene continues....

* * *

To explain that it was not the men who prepared the food, nor was there an artist making likenesses of those that were present sitting in the wings. The room was not ornate. It was a small room with very very sparse furnishings. What was placed on the table was what we could gather for it was a time of danger. The women were there and the children were there. Yes he did sit with the men and speak with

them, as was tradition but not to the exclusion of the
women who were at his side.   The gathering was
small, the room was small and not many knew of its
location. It was a High Holiday, it was Passover and it
was not taken lightly by any who were present.   It
commemorated an important time, one of great sacrifice and a time that required great faith.   So once
again they sat in great faith.

*   *   *

Mary of Bethany speaks -

*   *   *

And the ones who were there didn't know it was
the Last Supper. Yesh knew, I knew, the Magdalene
knew but the kind of knowing, the intuitive knowing,
again not knowing details but knowing down deep that
this was the end.   Some of the women were in the garden also; we both were there at a distance but none the
less there. (B)

*   *   *

*Mary Magdalene speaks of the Last Supper and
the Eucharist.*

*   *   *

Was it not even during that last celebration
together you refer to as supper that he said, "Take of
this and drink for it is my blood - eat of this for it is my
body"? So many ways this has been looked at, it has
been interpreted, it has been understood and it has
been misunderstood.   Again he was asking that those
who followed him embraced within them the same
Light that he carried to acknowledge that what they
had within them, their blood and their body was indeed
a vessel of Divine Light, the Christed Light, not the

Light of one man but the Light of the cosmos, of the universe, of the all. This is the message I bring - breathe it in, hold to heart the spark of divine Light that beats within you for the Light of God is in each one. And when you see the Light of God in your own eyes how easy to see it in each other. A new message? I think not. Does it need to be said again and again until every one on the face of this earth embraces *that* Light and no longer feels that they must stumble in a world of humanity, of darkness. Yes, it must be said again and so I have. (G)

* * *

Coming for Jesus in Gethsemane

The hours between the last meal Jesus had with his friends and the time he was taken by his enemies were spent in the Garden of Gethsemane. For those who knew what was to happen it must have been a very sad and fearful time. Mary tells of the power of this place.

* * *

My mind brings me to the Garden of Gethsemane. This is a place that has often been referred to but not nearly enough. They speak of it during the last days of Yeshua as a place that he went and he prayed with the others knowing the end would soon be coming and he knowing it was just a beginning. This sacred place was more than one stop in a lifetime. You speak of places of energy, powerful places on your planet for those of you that have interest. It is Gethsemane that has one of these powerful places. Indeed your entire world is one of God's Light and Love and

powerful in essence that it is.   But there are places on
your earth where the essence of the God Light of the
universal Light is felt more clearly with less effort raising the frequency of those who come lifting their hearts
and their minds.

Gethsemane was one of those places.   Yeshua
often brought us there for he was brought there as a
child.   Inquisitive, he played among the rocks and
among the trees, fascinated by the way they twisted
and turned, gnarled upon themselves.   Yet with all the
twists and turns that they had they were in essence
strong; growing straight from the earth, very much like
humanity.   In this place he felt the love of his father,
no, not a man sitting on a throne but the God Light,
the Universal Light, the consciousness of Love, the
eternal vibration that holds us all together, that is the
essence of all that is.   It is where he had come from,
remembering his soul's journey.

It was here that his soul lifted in joy and
reached out to the universe to hear and know what was
next to be.   He brought the others; he brought me and
often sat and talked about the mysteries and wonders
of the stars and skies and far beyond where the eye
could not see.   It was in this place that he spoke to us
of senses other than the five that we were using.   It
was in this place that he spoke to us of vision within
vision, a vision beyond vision, of knowing beyond
knowing.   It is not unusual that this would be the
place he would last choose to be.   It was here that he
asked for the guidance of the universe, of his guides
and guardians.   Yes, he had them, he did not walk
alone, nor did he stand alone.   I sat in quiet stillness,

which was hard for me, and I watched him. I remember his eyes looking toward me. I too, saw what was to be. John (the Divine) already knew, for Yeshua had shared with him already on a hillside but he chose to see no more.

The others were restless, uncomfortable in this place that had provided comfort all along. That restlessness was there, fighting against seeing and knowing, for each one could have turned to inner vision to know what would transpire over the next days but chose not to. It was their fear and their love and their doubt and their humanity that closed their eyes within their eyes. There is much to be learned. "When do they start trusting?" These were the words that were in my heart as I looked around me. Couldn't they all see what was to be? And beyond that, I could see where they were going for even before the moment of truth, they were fleeing and even now those who have the knowing, that are remembering, are fleeing from what they know. I bring not only what was but also messages of what can be or what will be during your lifetimes now. Trust and look inside to the great eternity within us, into the Light of your soul as he taught us. Do not fear what you see. Fear more of what you refuse to see. What you fear to see is more dangerous than the truth.

They came for him in the quiet of the night prepared for a battle, for a struggle, as though they had to trap him. Did they not know that he would go with them freely? There would be no running. He was treated as though there was a struggle and yet there was none. Many, stood aside, those names of which you read. Others, you do not hear of, went to his side, myself included.   It is with us that they had their battle, their struggle. I turned and looked and many were gone.   Thomas was gone, Luke was gone, Peter was gone. So many strange faces appeared out of the nothingness. So many familiar ones disappeared into the darkness.

Many of the women remained. In truth we had not much to fear. They did not think much of us as far as causing harm. And yet we held the same truth and the teachings of those they tried to entrap. It was the one time and the one moment that being a woman worked for us; for we were considered nothing. And many of us were the ones who quietly, in our homes and with our children, continued his words, his teachings. I do not denounce the men, they did what they must and there were many that finally stood up and spoke for truth. Fear not. But he taught us, the women, because he knew it was we that would teach the young children in the quiet of our homes. In our beds at night we would talk to them of the Light of their souls. Nothing could stop the whispers. So this is the way it was. (F)

*   *   *

Crucifixion and Resurrection

A woman asks, "Mary at the time of the crucifixion was Jesus held at an etheric level and then lowered back to his body at the end of three days? What went on between his physical body and his spiritual body at the time of the crucifixion?"

*   *   *

Indeed, what you asked is what you already know because Yeshua was both aware of his spirit and his humanity. He was able to go into both places. His humanity did experience all that was happening to him. The ability of his mind and his soul to move into that which was greater was able to give comfort. He heard the words of the universe always and at times when his body pulled him into his humanity more than spirit, he did cry out from that place and then move back into that place of spirit.

At the moment of his death, he stayed very close to his humanity, to his body; he did not ascend completely into Light although Light he was. His choice was to stay where his followers could experience, could see and could feel him before his final journey into the highest vibration of Light. He stayed close to the earth plane; his etheric body remained present. At the time, he appeared to me outside of the tomb, it was his etheric body that I was able to see. It was that body that was seen by those who followed him, by those who came, by those who were willing to see. And after he had spoken to those who needed to be spoken to, he moved into the next level of his spiritual body. The vibration moved even higher and he went into a different state of Light and to a higher state of Light. This is beginning to be understood by many. Yes, the etheric state was maintained and was felt and was seen and was heard. (J)

*   *   *

After His Death

Jesus' human existence was finished on the cross and his body was placed in a tomb. Traditional belief has told us its story about what happened and Mary of Bethany tells another.

Dr. Bezmen asks, "Can you share what happened after his death in the tomb?"

*   *   *

It is a very painful time to draw memory from. Suffice it to say that he was taken out of the tomb on Saturday evening and that the soldiers who guarded it were really followers who rolled back the stone and allowed him to be taken to a cave. This cave is near Jerusalem, the Essene women had prepared. When he was born a ritual began. There was a small stone altar made in the cave and every four hours two women came to that cave and they knelt in front of that altar and they sent him Light, surrounded him in Light.

That was the image they held from the day he was born until the day he died. Every four hours, the changing of the guard. And in the cave there were the vials where he was anointed properly and then he was buried, not in the tomb but in another place. (B)

*   *   *

Desecration of His Body Feared

*   *   *

We feared his desecration. There were many

that were looking for his body. There were many that wanted to destroy it further, that thought that death was not enough, that feared him so and of the power he had with people. We could not allow him to be desecrated any further so we took him to a place of safety. And yes, his spirit returned to us, his soul walked amongst us, appeared to many before it returned to his father, but we would not have him desecrated further. (B)

* * *

Resurrection

The story of the Resurrection has mystified and held the attention of believers for the past two thousand years. Mary is asked by Dr. Bezmen to explain more about the Resurrection.

* * *

There is much wonder as to what occurred in the resurrection of Yeshua. Some of what I say may be disturbing to some and others will find comfort in it. There was reality and also mystery and both can occupy the same moment. His resurrection has meaning to those that hold the vision in their hearts that life does not end, that spirit does not end, but is endless. That the energy of the soul and the Light of each one continues far beyond human existence, human flesh, the human body. He asked of the father of the universe, and of the guardians of Light and the Councils of Light, "How may I teach this? What may we bring to those that behold it that they will embrace into their hearts, the endlessness of life, of spirit, and of the great possibilities that they have available to them and that in spirit nothing is impossible." The resurrection of Yeshua was an example of this. First, I must say his body did not disappear from the tomb where it was placed. This is the clarity that I must bring to this situation.

We knew the guards. There were many guards that followed the words and the Love of Yeshua. The guards that stood at the cave knew that we must remove his body for it would have been desecrated. It was not in trickery or in deception that his body was removed but you must understand the times and what was happening to the people. His followers were in a panic. "How could this one we call God be dead? How could he have left if he was truly the God that we thought?" Such confusion and yet there were some, as myself, and some of the close followers that understood his words and understood that his humanity was to come to an end, although I did not wish it to be that way.

We went and we moved his body to a sacred place, a place; that he loved, a place that we were taught, a place where we endlessly sat and listened to the stories of Light, and of healing and of Love; the new ways and the laws that needed to be changed. It was here that we brought his body. The manifestation of the resurrection was palpable, felt as flesh. The spirit can move through dimension and time and as it does, meets with different frequencies and vibrations. This is the science of your times, concepts that were not understood by us then. As his soul essence returned to the earth and walked among those closest to him. The density of his energy become palpable, tangible. His resurrection was an apparition and an example of how spirit can move through time and space, how energy merely changes its density, its form but is eternal. It laid in many hearts as hope and faith of salvation and for those it gave comfort to and strengthened the Light of God. This was good, not entirely the intent, but this was good. Not the intent to elevate himself to a god, but to a magnificent part of God's Light, as all are. Does that make sense? (D)

*　*　*

Joseph of Arimathea and the Shroud of Turin

The Church has made many uses of relics to convince our humanity of the truth of Jesus' existence. The Shroud of Turin has been one relic that repeatedly captures the attention of both those who believe and those who doubt. Mary of Bethany was asked about this sacred cloth.

Dr. Bezmen asks, "There is a lot of controversy about an artifact called the Cloth of Turin. Have either one of you heard of it and can you shed any Light on it?"

Mary of Bethany answers...

*　*　*

Yes. You have heard of Joseph of Arimathea who was the uncle of Yeshua. He was a very wealthy man and it was he who traveled with Yesh. It was he who took him to all of those places and in his travels he acquired many things and one of them was a cloth.

When he (Jesus), was taken down from the cross he was laid on that cloth. It was put over him and he was carried away. But he was not wrapped up in it in the tomb. He was taken to a place where he was very quickly cleaned up and anointed before sundown and then he was placed in the tomb. And the cloth was placed there with him, as were all of the oils that were used. That artifact is real. It will never be proven so, in the immediate future, because it is alive and always changing. Someday people will know. (B)

* * *

CHAPTER THIRTEEN

The Second Coming

"Do we believe in a self destructive God or do we believe in an everlasting Light? Every time someone questions and calls upon the Truth, the Light, and the Universal Love that flows through them; it is the Second Coming. Every time even one soul recognizes their connection to another; it is the Second Coming. Destruction is a choice of humanity, not a choice of God."

The New Testament speaks of the Second Coming and each sect of the Christian family of religions has interpreted it in their own way. The concept has given hope of better times and a belief in ultimate justice. In the past many have asserted that tomorrow, next month or within the next five years we would witness this world changing event. This has not occurred. Two thousand years have passed and we are still waiting. Is it possible that our understanding is flawed and that the Second Coming is not a single or future event, but a continuous and timeless offering of the spirit?

The Magdalene elaborates on the truth of the Second Coming.

*   *   *

The truth is the Christ energy has come and gone many times. The Christed energy has flowed through the span of time, dimension after dimension, bringing with it the truth of Light and the choice of receiving it. Will there be widespread destruction of humanity as some speak of it? Would the hand of God be so angry as to cut down His own people; the Light that is part of the whole? For God to be angered and to destroy the Light of even one man, is to destroy His own Light and a part of Himself. Do we believe in a self destructive God, or an ever lasting Light? Every time someone questions and calls upon the Truth, the Light, and the universal Love that flows through them, it is the Second Coming. Every time even one soul recognizes their connection to another, it is the Second Coming. Destruction is a choice of humanity, not a choice of God. (C)

There have been questions that I hear spoken in

your time, actually throughout time, words of the Second Coming. And I have discussed this with you before; I have shared with my heart, with my words. He will not appear before you as a human in a solid form as a reincarnation whole and intact on a chariot of fire or any other vehicle of your time. Instead, he bursts forth with so much Light and so much love that part of this Light showers down upon you. So much of this Light is shared in each soul, in each heart and in each Light, even those who sit before me now. Yes, he comes again. The consciousness, the word, the truth, the love, the compassion and the knowing.

The link between the heavens and earth, the bridge between sanity and insanity, that which sometimes is so frail between joy and sorrow. His Light shines down and scatters like stardust on your earth. For now is the time when so much healing is needed of the people, of the planet; of all living things that surround you, that support you, that comfort you, that reach to you in the quiet of night and the brightest of the day. Yes, there is a Second Coming and a third and a fourth and as many times and as many numbers as far reaching as the universe. That is how many times the Word of God, of the Universe, of Source, of One, of all the terms that are used throughout the ages, as infinite as that, is the infinite amount of times that he will return and speak.

He speaks through the smile of a child, through the weathered skin of the frailest of the old. He speaks in a touch, he speaks without touch. He teaches always that the Light that you seek and the comfort that you long for is in you and around you. It holds you, it supports you and it is present for you. It is the well, like the well I stood by so many thousands of years ago, a well without a bottom, a well that never empties, that never runs dry.   For as long as there is breath, there is hope and peace. Where there is life, there is the Presence of the Universe. (D)

*   *   *

Dr. Bezmen asks, "Does Yeshua ever manifest in our earth plane to bring a message and then leave?"

*   *   *

Yes.   I smile because as he sits with us now he is delighted.   He, as many of Light, can manifest in physical form.   It is this movement through energy fields and dimensions that I speak of.   As he would say, if he appeared as Christ before someone who was in need, more times than not, he would frighten them. They would not believe what they saw, or worse yet, feel they were unworthy to see what they were seeing.   Very often he comes in the physical presence of men and women.   The energy of his Light shining through their eyes, speaking the truths, the words of comfort, of guidance that is needed at that time.

But you must understand further that what he does, he does in the Light of God and that each soul, each spark of Light, each presence in this room comes in as the Light of God, the Christed Light, into humanity now. For when he refers to his Christed Light, he smiles for in definition the Christed Light is the Light of God as it shines through the experience of humanity.

Yes, he shows himself, of late, he enjoys what you refer to as jeans.   Many people, especially young people find comfort in this man looking quite unpretentious in jeans, with eyes that are like the deepest seas or the vastness of the stars and love pouring out of his heart and hands. How many healers lay hands upon those people they touch and Yeshua embraces them and together they work the Light of God in that healing. He is present in many ways. (D)

* * *

Mary of Bethany speaks of the Second Coming...

* * *

We speak of the Second Coming, we hear of the Second Coming all the time. But Yeshua will not come back as a man, as a god in the form of a single person. His Second Coming will be when his soul essence shines out from every human being; when we look at another human being and see Christ, the Christ Light in that person. What is happening now is that more and more people are recognizing the Christ Light in themselves and in other people and the numbers will grow and grow and grow. And that is the Second Coming.

* * *

Dr. Bezmen asks, "This is not to be confused with all becoming Christians ?" and Mary of Bethany answers.. * * * **No** * * *

The Magdalene continues...

* * *

But the Christ Light being a representation of the Light of God that shined in one man so brightly that for decades of time it would not die. You may find that Light in a Buddhist, you may find that Light in a Muslim, you may find that Light in every "primitive", as you would say, religion and culture, in the heart of every shaman who gives glory to God, the Source, by honoring all living things. That is the Christ Light.(B

* * *

Dr. Bezmen inquires, "Mary, would there be a point when mass consciousness would raise our vibrations and the holy Christ body would enter within and around our flesh?"

* * *

Yes. And it is proper for you to ask this question. It is your soul and your consciousness raising out and reaching for what, in essence, you already know. He spoke the words, "Take of this for this is my body." Has the meaning changed in that, as many of his words were heard differently by so many.? If they listened with their hearts they would understand that the consciousness that he held, the vibration that he held, the Light that he remembered can indeed be taken into this body that you possess, into this incarnation, into the being of your self. You may lift and raise your body with the consciousness of the Christed one.

Yes, the time will come when the souls remember, and the hearts remember, and embrace that which he spoke of, that which he prophesied. Yes, it is at hand for those who will receive it, for those who embrace it, for those who do not fear to ask what you have asked. It is at hand for those who dare to look with eyes and hear with ears that lie within, and that feel with the essence of the universe, what is truth. Yes, great changes will take place for more have embraced his words, some without even knowing what his words were, some hearing them in the way they were translated; but still knowing that the essence of these words held something more. Look beyond words; feel, sense and know. Look into that Light, really surrender to the Light of the universe. So you are already more than you know! (F)

* * *

The Second Coming

CHAPTER FOURTEEN

The Council of Light

> "The Council of Light is
> that part of consciousness of
> pure Light, of pure Love, of wis-
> doms and knowledge of all that
> has passed before you."

Most of us, in our lives, have had the over-whelming feeling that we were alone no matter how many other people were physically nearby. Even the holy ones, the spiritually focused, the mystics of all religions have shared that they too have had that feeling, if only momentarily. Jesus, on the cross, questioned his being forsaken by God. Those feelings seem universal in our human existence. The depressive state we find ourselves in when having such feelings suggests that this is not normal, this is not the way. Spiritual alone-ness and separation is not what life should be. Is there only us here and God there, or are there other spirits who are not in physical reality working with us, cheering for our growth and giving us comfort? Mary says that such compassionate energies do exist and are as near as we allow them to be.

Explanation of the Council

Dr. Bezmen asks, "Mary, I have a question. We have often heard of the Council of Light or the Great Council. How did Yeshua and how do you explain that council? Can you share your understanding of it?"

* * *

Follow with me for all of you are my brothers and sisters of Light. The Council of Light is not a group of spirits cloaked in shimmering cloth sitting behind a large pedestal of Light. However, these are the images that help your humanity understand the workings and the power of spirit so it is not wrong to image it in this way. But know it does not exist in that manner.

The Council of Light

We are all part of immense Light, Light that has no beginning and no end. These words have been heard since the beginning of time and are yet so difficult to embrace. So small is humanity that this concept does not fit in us. Yet, so great is our spirit in that Light that there is division, but not in the constructs of the mind as you see it. There are aspects of consciousness way beyond your present understanding.

Think of your thoughts and of your emotions. Is there a wall between one thought and another? Is there division? Can you not go from laughter to tears without barrier between them but yet there is a separateness? So is the collective consciousness of Light. Separate, but without boundaries as you would see it.

The Council of Light is that part of consciousness of Light of pure Love, of wisdoms and knowledge of all that has passed before you; and in that part of Light, decisions are made. The decision to come to flesh, and the decision of spirit to manifest into flesh are examples. They are the keepers of the purpose of Light and of Love. Many aspects of consciousness are brought back to the Light by the experiences of humanity. It is the Great Council that sorts these knowledges, sorts these experiences and places universal order and perfection on all that pass through Light.

Difficult to understand, but not as difficult as you may make it. Just like loving yourself; allow the understanding and the peace of that understanding to settle within you and do not struggle against it. Is it not easier to float in the stream of life than to be battling up the waterfalls; the waterfalls that you see, that you fight so hard against! Rather, allow yourself to float freely and there will be another for you to experience, another place that you can flow into. There is too much struggle! Allow yourselves to be and invite the visions to come and so they will. (C)

*   *   *

Guardians of Light as Teachers

*   *   *

The guides, as you call them, the guardians of Light, come here for purpose, each one with a teaching, with a lesson, each one with information that can help you on your journey, not merely in this lifetime but in your soul's passage through the universe of Light. (F)

*   *   *

The "Light One"

The Council of Light as explained by Mary is a spiritual group consciousness. Within that consciousness are sparks of Divine Light that have individual connections to mankind, yet are inseparable from the whole.

Dr. Bezmen asks about the "Light One". "We have been getting impressions from the energy known as the "Light One" and I was wondering if you could translate the message that she wants us to hear now or that group of souls desires?"

*   *   *

I may speak of "her" although she has no gender. She is of the stars, the Universe, of Pleiades and beyond the Pleiades. She travels in more than one dimension and has been known by many in many ways. She is the essence of Light, a spark that has healed and has brought many universes together. This energy is the ribbon of Light that weaves from one nation to another, from one people to another. It was her energy, her beautiful essence, that danced in the heart of Yeshua as he laid his hands upon those that were ill. It was the nurturing, mothering energy, that which you call matriarchal, that passed through him; her essence that drew each person into his heart. It was this tiny spark of Light who speaks to me now. This energy coming close within me and very much a part of me is combining the energies, all energy is to heal and to create. It is the essence of life.

Many have asked, "How is life begun, what is creation?" It is tiny sparks of vibrant Light, so small that the eye can not see a fraction of the star. It is what makes the stars twinkle and shine. Can you see the part that is written (in the stars)? Take a fragment of translucency and the Light Ones are there. It is this tiny energy of Light that can create, that pulls together, that brings together the cells of the beings of the humanity. It is the communication between each cell, each spark of Light inside of you, and each piece of radiance within you.

Each tiny part of us can be transmitted from one to another as you lay your hands and eyes and send the Light from one being to another. Tiny impulses of this Light communicate and know what is needed. In many ways we are faster than Light, energy that is beyond that speed. Some have seen us as tracers, known as little bits of Light.   We are not separate but working together and there are billions of us.   We are the Light Ones and I speak collectively of us.   Feel us in the tips of your fingers, in the Lightest touch.   It is known by your humanity.   It is like tiny wisps, almost unfelt but yet felt very powerfully. Healing of this planet and the universe lays in each one of you.   You are not separate, though you try to be; as tiny as a speck of this twinkling Light that I speak of. That is sometimes how you feel in the universe; as though you can not be seen.

You can, and as a collective, as I speak to you now, join together; each one of your sparks to become those tracers of Light, seeing, creating a web of Light around your planet.   Seen are these tracers to other galaxies and planets, and so it continues.   Each part is sent, each part alive and radiant.   Atlanteans were comprised primarily of chains of these Lights.   You can think that we are like the DNA that created "Light bodies" before the denser energies came. (L)

*   *   *

The Council of Light

CHAPTER   FIFTEEN

September 13, 2001

"Peace is a gift that comes from true understanding. From true understanding grows compassion. From compassion, there is only love. Be in love. We will not desert you."

Magdalene speaks two days after September 11th.

* * *

It is through the veil of tears and pain that we come toward this time.   Have no doubt that you have not been abandoned by all the legions of Light, by the angels of Light, by the powers of Love in the universe.   It is easy to look towards that which has been lost and allow the pain and fear to rise within you. I can not deny you that and we do not deny that but take comfort and look towards the Love that has risen through the ashes - look at the Lights of so many that have rushed forward without thought of themselves to reach to another brother and sister in Light.

Yes, the pain is deep, the grief unbearable, but the love, the courage, the faith that rises from the hearts of so many are all around you now.   Choose what you want to look at.   Be careful where your heart leads you.   Let not your heart lead you in that place of fear and hatred, that created that which is now. I do not have to tell you that this is not the first time that life has been lost in the name of what is truth, God, belief, but know from where it comes.   Be seekers of truth and Light and look beyond the deeds and words, look through the tears and sorrow and see the root of this evil.   Look for the shadows, you will see fear beyond fear.   You will see hatred beyond hatred.   To think the same is to create the same.   There were those, at the time that I walked, that cried out for revenge of Yeshua's death; that screamed out, "Kill those responsible!"   And in many ways this came to pass; rumblings, plottings, revenge, hatred, and fear. His word did not survive nor did love grow from being in those places. The enemy was not crushed with hatred and as you see the fear and doubt, the judgement of one another has not changed through the times when banners were carried in his name and men and women and children were slaughtered. Did those times eradicate the anger and hate, the anger and hatred you see before you now? Or did fear create more; did anger create itself over and over again?

It is difficult to ask you to be in a place of Love at this time, to ask you to be in a place of peace, to feel the presence of God and the Light. To know that cries were heard, to believe that this was not a punishment or abandonment by all the highest beings of Light. These acts were not ones of Spirit, of Divine Light, but that of humanity of which each one of you were given the gift. It is difficult to ask yourself to understand why any man, woman or child would use that gift of life to create death and fear. I do not speak to you from a place of Spirit but from a woman who walked your path; who knew shadow and sunlight, who knew joy and grief, who tasted anger and fear - anger and fear that raged inside of my body, the tears that were like razors in my eyes, that ripped at my heart and the hearts of so many. You cry out for his Light that was in each one of your brothers and sisters, that moved from their bodies into Light.

For those who loved them and know of their fate and those who still do not know and scream even in their sleep; if you can feel their pain and send your love from your heart, then you carry his words - you carry his truth - his Light; this is what he asked of us. This connection, this knowing that whatever happens to any one of us happens to all of us. And no one is alone. Yes, you can choose to be in fear, to wrap yourself up in hatred and anger and serve no one, not even yourself. But I ask what good will come of this? So much Love and Light in your hearts. It is there. It screams out, reaching to those you know and those you do not know, or do you?

Fear, anger, and hatred rise from not understanding at all. It comes from a place that hears only words; words alone will not change what is happening to humanity. It is only the gift and power of your faith and your love that can shine brighter than any fire; that can burn brightly through all darkness. Choose it now. I do not ask you to embrace those who have acted in such an unthinkable way. It is too painful now and that is your humanity and by that you will not be judged. Send instead the compassion that bursts from your heart.

We are watching and holding you all. We who have been in humanity know the pain and the fear that ripples across you in waves. Call out now! We will be there. Call to what you believe to be Light, I do not care by what name. Call out to the only power that can change or bring you into a place of growing peace. Many will follow many paths. You will see this. It was the same then; those that continued to refuse to believe what they saw before them, choosing to close their hearts and their minds, hiding even from themselves and their pain; those who angered and retaliated and raged inside; and those who continued to move forward refusing their Light to be put out. Was it not in the great city that the oil continued to be and burn in the lamps showing the presence of Light to the people of God? Your

Light is without beginning and without end. Choose to hold it before you.

The children are watching you, the children of your world listen to you, hear your words, feel your pain. What will you have them learn; hatred, fear? Will you teach them fear even now or will you teach them love? Will you show them that this is what comes to the heart that does not love? Can you teach them that this rose from fear; fear of loss, and fear of overpowerment? Can you teach them that this came from mistrust? Can you teach them now that those that created such pain, in truth, had lost their connection to God and when that Light went out so did the Light in their hearts for each other? For they love each other no more than they love you. Begin to rise from these ashes, steady your own truth and Light, be of one heart; there is such great power. Thousands have perished in the flesh and risen into Light. One hundred fold times that number and more have lit candles and prayed and held each other in love. See that now. Find comfort in that now. The time of darkness has not ended. The Divine Light of the beings of Light, of the master teachers of Light share with me now in truth that this has not ended. There can be no lies in pure Light.

Ripples of anger and fear continue to move through your people. In truth, others are gathering in more anger and hatred as we speak. It is not the destruction of your world, but others are to transition; more life will be lost, even those who caused this atrocity to man, their lives will be lost. Should you not even cry at the loss of their lives, at the sadness? Their time was not spent knowing the joy of Light. They will not know that joy as they pass through the veil of time. Those who embrace Light now will find healing and comfort. Those who caused this disaster will not and they are as much a part of you as those that you love. Many will die that hold no responsibility to this. All beings of Light grieve this as well. Light must prevail. Each one must hold it closely now. Each tear is yours and ours. We embrace you. Do not ask if you are heard. Know that you are, and prayers are being answered in ways that are beyond the comprehension of humanity. The loving God did not create this as a test of your faith. No being of Light creates darkness to show its own Light. Know this to be truth.

Please, Dear Ones of Light, know that you are held now, turn to one another just as we turned to one another then. When you feel your Light beginning to dim, when the fear feels like it is choking you, look to one who can hold you at this time. Do not stop the Light. Send it to them. There are many who are grieving beyond grief now. Embrace them as your own. Do not fall to the words, "I did not loose anybody in this disaster", for you did; you lost one of God's Lights - part of yourself. Do not loose your faith with them. Know that their faith burns strong and bright and that the love that you sent them is returning to you stronger and brighter than ever before on this planet.

Peace is a gift that comes from true understanding. From true understanding grows compassion. From compassion there is only love. Be in love. We will not desert you.

*   *   *

September 13, 2001

Afterword

The story that the Magdalene has given us of Jesus is the most human one I have heard. There is never the feeling that her Yeshua is the same master planner and messiah that was the focus of my early Christian education. In that training I was given the following image to believe in -

- Jesus was the only son of God who came into human existence differently than any of us.
- He was divine from the beginning and knew what he was about; no questions, no doubts.
- He was the promised one who would be persecuted and his life sacrificed as atonement for original sin.

I didn't find that Jesus in the Magdalene's telling of the story. What I did find was a man called Jesus who was fully human yet spiritually evolved. A man that questioned much, not only of the world around him but also of himself and what he believed. A man who took a different path, who studied all that he could of the spiritual and shared what he found with others. He was a seeker of truth who was willing to share a few simple messages :

- Love God with your whole being.
- Love one another for we are all brothers and sisters
- Live compassionately without judgement.
- Fully embrace your humanity.
- The kingdom of God is within you.

These, I believe, to be the essence of his teachings. Certainly my early religious education was much more detailed and complicated than these teachings.

The information that came through in these fifteen sessions, since 1995, has had a real impact on those who put this book together. Each of us had our own spiritual beliefs and this information made us wrestle with those beliefs. I imagine those readers who seriously consider the material in this book will be, at first, as unsettled as were we. Each of us has to personally decide what is our truth. The very definition of belief is that its validity can not be logically proved but rather, belief is what one decides to be true. All traditional belief systems that deal with spirit, divinity and miracles are in the same category,: that is, they can not be logically proved. So if what has been presented in this book is "true" for you, as it is for many of us, how has it challenged your former belief system? Can the Jesus introduced here sustain your spiritual needs and provide for spiritual growth? Can the Divine in each of us be cultivated as it was in Jesus if we follow his teachings?

Ed Stringham

"This is not Finished"

Appendix

*The channeled material in this book was tran-
scribed from fifteen sessions which took place over a
four and a half year period. A letter was assigned to
each of those sessions and was placed in parentheses at
the end of each section in the book. The list below shows
the dates represented by each of those letters.*

(A) FEB 6, 1997

(B) APRIL 11, 1997

(C) SEP 17, 1998

(D) MAY 7, 1999

(E) MAY 27, 1999

(F) JULY 23,1999

(G) SEP 2, 1999

(H) FEB 27, 2000

(I) MAR 1, 2000

(J) MAY 12, 2000

(K) SEP 7, 2000

(L) DEC 14, 2000

(M) MAR 15, 2001

(N) JUN 14, 2001

(O) SEP 13, 2001

This book may be ordered from -

STILL SMALL VOICE PUBLISHING
PO BOX 25
EAST BETHANY, NEW YORK
14054

for $17.95 (US) plus sales tax if sent to a New York state addre
Payment may be made by check or money order.
If ordered from SSV Publishing shipping and handling charge
are included.

This book may also be ordered from -

PATHWAYS TO HEALTH
77 SHORE DRIVE
MT. SINAI, NEW YORK
11766

toll free 1-866-597-2200
www.pathwaystohealth.com

- and at **Amazon. com**